Afterlife

What Really Happens on the Other Side

True Stories of Contact and Communication with Spirits

Barry R. Strohm

Dedication

While many people contributed to the writing of this book, there are only two persons without whom I could not have completed it.

The first of these individuals is my clairvoyant friend, Barbara Lee. Her unique ability to communicate with the spirits on the other side has been astounding and she indeed can talk to the angels. As you read this book, you will understand that she is a unique and blessed individual.

The other person instrumental to the completion of this book is my soulmate and wife of forty-eight years, Connie. Her inspiration and editing help has given me the strength to complete this latest look at the afterlife. She patiently attends all our sessions and tries her best not to fall asleep while listening to my presentations, which she has heard many times. When we channel, she takes notes and helps us understand the messages of the Spirit Guides. I have no doubt that when this life is over for us, we will come back some time in the future, together again.

Schiffer Books are available at special discounts for bulk purchases for sales promotions or premiums. Special editions, including personalized covers, corporate imprints, and excerpts can be created in large quantities for special needs. For more information contact the publisher:

Published by Schiffer Publishing, Ltd.
4880 Lower Valley Road
Atglen, PA 19310
Phone: (610) 593-1777; Fax: (610) 593-2002
E-mail: Info@schifferbooks.com

For the largest selection of fine reference books on this and related subjects, please visit our website at:
www.schifferbooks.com.

We are always looking for people to write books on new and related subjects. If you have an idea for a book, please contact us at:
proposals@schifferbooks.com.

This book may be purchased from the publisher.
Please try your bookstore first.
You may write for a free catalog.

Contents

Acknowledgments

As you read this book, you will come to realize that many events had to take place to lead me to the information and tools that would allow me to live these often unbelievable events. Without Steve McNaughton and the Paranormal Environmental Explanations from Research (P.E.E.R) paranormal investigation group, I would have never been introduced to the earthbound ghosts that inhabited my business, Golden Lane Antique Gallery, in New Oxford, Pennsylvania. Steve also introduced me to Barbara Lee, my clairvoyant friend who opened the doors to spirit communication.

My friends in Utah introduced me to the spirit or talking board. This device enabled us to receive messages from the spirits, clearly spelled out in detail. Carol Green founded the Ray of Light Research Center over forty years ago in Salt Lake City, Utah. She is also the author of *You, and Your Board of Guides*, a collection of channeling notes collected over many years that I have learned from and used as a reference in this book. Carol and her partner, Laurie Kelley, along with K and Doc Kivet and Sammi Tall, were kind enough to introduce me to their unique method of contacting the spirit world.

I would also like to give special thanks to my ghost friends, Jeffery Silverman and Bert Connely. Their contributions to our paranormal sessions have been crucial to introducing our guests to the wonders of the spirit world. In addition, they have given us detailed information about Connie and my prior lives. As you will see, I have devoted a chapter to each of these special spirits.

Epigraph

One evening we were channeling in Utah and these words
of advice were given to us by the Spirit Guides:

Message For All

Life is a gift.
You can enjoy it, embrace it.
Yes, and want more.
Or you can fight it, fear it, and make everyone hate you, but it is your choice.
You make it what you want it to be

Introduction

For the purpose of this book, I am defining the afterlife as what happens when the soul passes from this incarnate life, or death of the body. I have been told there are over 11,000 religions in the world that translates into over 11,000 definitions of what happens after death. Along with my friend, Barbara Lee, we have been given the gift of communication with the spirits of deceased souls and the Heavenly guides. They have given us insights into not only the existence of an afterlife, but details of what really takes place on the other side of the veil of life. I maintain audio and video recordings of all the described events as irrefutable proof of the happenings that occurred in this book.

This book is a collection of true short stories that tell of the events that led me from a total disregard for the spirit world to a life of teaching others about what happens after the soul leaves the body in death. As you read of my personal journey, you will learn that death is the beginning, not the end of your journey on a Karma path. I have also included specific information about subjects such as improving your paranormal photography, making and using a "Ghost Box," removing evil spirits from a home, and many more subjects related to learning about and experiencing the afterlife or communicating with the other side while still here on earth.

Many readers are familiar with the presence of earthbound spirits or ghosts, but few are familiar with the different types of Heaven-bound spirits that influence our lives on a daily basis. Most notable are the Spirit Guides that allow direct communication with the other side. In Chapter 9: There is More to Life, the difference between earthbound ghosts and Heaven-bound spirits, or guides, is explained in the exact transcribed words of the Heavenly guides. I have even included the picture of a real angel, lifting the body of a soldier off the battlefield in Gettysburg.

My stories delve into all aspects of the afterlife, from whether there really is a "Hell" to the actual quotes of spirits that relate what happens upon death. In one story, I recount the details of a Confederate colonel that is still fighting the battle of Gettysburg and is not aware he has passed. Included in that chapter is a picture of the ghost of the Confederate soldier, still fighting in the afterlife. Another story tells of an interview with the spirit of Ulysses S. Grant in which the general and past president of the United States relates his appreciation for the manner in which he is being portrayed by living history re-enactors.

One evening Barbara Lee and I were channeling with a General Guide and I mentioned that we were on an amazing journey. The guide replied:

Yes, you are.

I hope you will join us on this amazing journey as we explore the miracle of life after death and what really happens in the afterlife

Glossary

Afterlife Upon death, your soul passes from your incarnate life into another dimension or realm and continues to exist in that dimension. The belief in life after death.

Angel A celestial being that acts as an intermediary in carrying out the wishes of God.

Apparition A state in which a spirit may be seen as they were in life. They may be seen as full bodied or in a partial form. For instance, a floating head.

Channeling A method of spirit communication in which a medium or person sensitive to receiving spirit messages relays direct messages from those souls in the afterlife.

Channeling Board A printed board with numerals, letters, phrases, and words to receive the messages from souls in the afterlife. A planchette or glass pointer will move to the letters or numbers to spell out specific messages. Also referred to as a "talking board," "spirit board," or Ouija board.

Clairvoyant An individual with the ability to see and communicate with the spirits in the afterlife through mental imagery or an intuitive process.

Demon An evil deity or spirit. They are capable of possessing a human, creating destructive acts, and leading individuals to live outside religious guidelines.

Earthbound Spirit A spirit that has either been unable to move on or has made the decision to remain in the Earth plane.

Ectoplasm A fog-like mist that is associated with spirit hauntings. When photographed, the cloud-like form may take the appearance of angels, human forms, or even vortexes. It is a cloud of spirit energy, also referred to as plasma.

EMF Meter An electronic device that measures Electromagnetic force. An earthbound spirit presence will often emit an electromagnetic force.

Exorcism A ritual to remove an evil entity from a location, person, or even an animal. Generally religious in nature, a qualified person or priest will call upon a higher deity to cast out the evil presence.

Free Will In each incarnate lifetime, the soul is given the ability to make its own decisions concerning their life path. The decision to follow an evil path is always made in this side of the life veil.

Ghost A general term that refers to the presence of a supernatural entity. It typically refers to the presence of an apparition, but it can take the form of a shadow figure or ectoplasm form.

Ghost Box An electronic instrument, generally a modified radio that rapidly scans the wavelengths to create a background noise that allows the spirits use the energy and verbally communicate to humans.

Guardian Angel A spiritual or celestial being specifically assigned to protecting an individual in time of harm.

Guide Heavenly spirits that provide spiritual energy to help humans learn in order to progress along their Karma path. The energy to learn is provided to an individual from the womb to death by these spirits. There are guides for all purposes, such as writing, learning, walking, and all other human functions.

Heaven The highest of the realms; the location of the throne of God, holy angels, and special individuals, such as Saints who have attained spiritual purity. A place to be obtained by believers only after the return of Christ.

Hell A place of punishment where the soul is sent after death.

Incarnate Life The period from birth to death when a soul occupies a physical body.

Intelligent Haunting Supernatural events by spirits that retain the ability to reason and respond to specific requests.

K2 Meter A specific type of electromagnetic force meter that has small lights to reflect the intensity of the EMF signal.

Karma The belief that events in your prior life have an effect on your present life. For example, if an individual was evil in their past life, events will occur to punish them in their current life.

Karma Path At the time a soul enters an incarnate lifetime, events in your prior life created a pre-ordained path.

Medium An individual with clairvoyant abilities who acts as an intermediary between a third party and the spirit world to deliver messages.

Orb A spirit orb is the form most often taken by the soul while in the earthbound dimension. The size and color of the ball-like shape can vary greatly. When photographed with a fast shutter speed, the facial image of the spirit can often be seen.

Paranormal A paranormal event is some type of experience or happening that is outside the normal range of happenings and defies scientific explanation.

Prior Life The belief that your soul existed in an earlier lifetime. Your soul may have experienced prior lives over thousands of years.

Psychic A psychic is a person who has the ability to display paranormal powers. Psychic powers can range from the ability to see and communicate with spirits to an extrasensory perception to predict the future.

Purgatory A concept generally associated with the Catholic Church. A place where the soul goes after death to undergo purification before gaining access to Heaven.

Reincarnation The ability of a soul to return after biological death to a new life as the soul attempts to gain experience toward obtaining higher realms in the afterlife.

Séance A gathering of individuals with a medium in order to receive messages or communications from spirits of the dead or Heavenly guides. A channeling session is a type of séance.

Sensitive The ability to sense or feel paranormal activity.

Shadow People A type of apparition in which the entity takes the form of a shadow as opposed to a full-body form. Generally, there is no recognizable form. Often seen as movement out of the corner of your eye.

Soul The immortal energy of an individual. Upon death, the soul energy leaves the body to embark on another journey of learning experiences.

Spirit A spirit is the unique energy that grows from the personification of a human being. The spirit is the presence that appears after death while the soul moves on in eternal life.

Spirit Attachment A spirit may choose to remain with an object or person to which it was attracted in life. For instance, an oil painting that depicted the image of the person may have the spirit remain attached to the object.

Spirit Board A specific type of talking board designed to communicate with the Heavenly guides. It consists of numbers, letters, and words used to deliver specific messages. It has a glass top and uses a glass pointer or planchette.

Spirit Photography A special type of photography to record paranormal activity. Infrared and ultraviolet light may be used to record all areas of the spectrum.

Spirit Possession The act by which a spirit or demon takes over the body of an individual.

Supernatural An act unexplainable by science or natural law, often attributed to God or a deity.

Trance An altered state of consciousness other than normal waking, such as hypnosis.

Unknowing Dead A channel or dimension where the spirit is not aware it has passed from the living. For instance, soldiers may still be fighting as they did in life.

Chapter 1

Reason to Believe

When individuals tell me they are skeptics, my normal answer is that I was a major skeptic for the first sixty years of my life. My scientific background cried out that there could never be ghosts or a life after death. If you can't see "it" or touch "it," surely "it" cannot exist. While I have always considered myself spiritual, the idea that an individual could actually see and communicate with the spirits of the deceased or Heavenly guides was a concept beyond my wildest imagination.

Golden Lane Antique Gallery, located in New Oxford, Pennsylvania. Dating to 1877, when it was a shoe factory, the store has a large and very active spirit presence.

In the late 1980s, I purchased an abandoned 30,000-square-foot shoe factory in New Oxford, Pennsylvania, with the intent of creating an antique gallery. The building dated back to the 1870s, when a thriving shoe industry was the mainstay for the area. In my wildest dreams, I did not realize at the time that I was purchasing a condominium for ghosts. I remodeled the building for the sale of art and antiques and Golden Lane Antique and Art Gallery became a successful destination for customers from all parts of the country. A management staff took care of the store as I pursued other interests as an absentee owner. During the early years of owning the store, my employees would talk of strange happenings. Whenever I heard their stories, I would laugh them off as being impossible. By 2005, my situation changed and I began to spend more time at the antique gallery.

Footsteps Overhead, EMF Recordings, and Photos

Whenever I was present at the store, the staff told me of the sound of footsteps on the floor overhead, lights being turned on during the night, shadow figures looking over customers' shoulders, and finding locked doors to utility closets. My comments whenever I heard the stories were that my staff should spend less time at the bars or change what they were smoking—or maybe even both. Customers came to the checkout desk and asked if we knew there were ghosts in the building. Usually, they would say not to worry since they were friendly. I figured the customers were hanging out at the bars with my staff.

Several years ago, one of my employees asked permission to come into the store at night and try to get pictures of the ghosts. My exact answer was: "Knock yourself out." Little did I know that what happened to my employee would actually change the direction and belief structure for the remainder of my life. When I came into the store a couple of days later, she could hardly wait to tell me about what happened.

My employee and her friend went to the store one night after dark, armed with a tape recorder, an EMF (electromagnetic force) meter, and a camera. (At the end of this chapter, I will include a section describing how to effectively use an EMF meter.) When they entered the store, she turned on the tape recorder and put it in her pocket. The recorder captured the sounds of everything that happened that night. As we listened to the events of the evening, you could clearly hear the sound of the two individuals walking up the back stairs. When they approached the door at the top of the stairs, the EMF meter began to make a beeping sound, clearly heard on the recorder, indicating a possible spirit presence.

As we listened to the recording, their voices became excited as they discussed the prospect of why the meter was beeping and what was behind the door. As they opened the door, the recorder clearly caught my employee's voice exclaiming, "There she is and she's smiling." The next words were spoken by her friend as she posed the question, "May we take your picture?" To my surprise, the recorder picked up a low, but clear, "Yes." A flash picture was taken in response to the permission given by the ghost.

The next sound heard on the recorder was my employee uttering in a panicked voice: "She is coming toward us." All you could hear at this time was the sound of footsteps

A professional investigator is photographed in a mirror at Golden Lane Antique Gallery. Note there is no evidence of a spirit presence behind the investigator.

running down the stairs as though attempting to get out of the store as rapidly as possible. Apparently, the informal investigation had come to an abrupt and unanticipated ending. Neither of them suggested they go back into the store to try to continue their paranormal experience.

As soon as we finished listening to the recording, my employee pulled out her camera and displayed the image that was taken in the store on the night of her adventure. The camera had clearly recorded the ectoplasm form of the head and shoulders of a person. You could see the shape of eyes and a smiling mouth! Additionally, you could see the antiques in the aisle of the upper level of our store *through* the misty form. In the past, I had always doubted the authenticity of this type of ghost picture, but I also knew these individuals had no reason to make up the story. I also realized they did not know how to use PhotoShop! In this instance, there was little doubt. There really were ghosts residing at Golden Lane Antique Gallery!

The next evening, in an effort to verify the spiritual presence recorded by my employees, I went through the store in the dark with my digital flash camera taking multiple pictures. In several of the pictures, there were some very bright orbs. I had always believed orbs were either light reflected from dust or water particles. When I enlarged the images of the orbs, I found that some even had faces in them! I decided to bring in a professional group of paranormal investigators to verify the existence of the ghosts.

We approached Steve McNaughton, an author of paranormal books and the head of the Paranormal Environmental Explanations from Research (P.E.E.R.) paranormal group, to conduct an investigation of the store. The investigation revealed multiple proofs of our ghost population, but one group of photographs in particular solidified my belief in the spirit world.

During the session, one of the investigators noted that there was movement of a hanging lamp in an area of the store. Several of the investigators entered the booth and a series of photographs were taken in an effort to determine what caused the movement of the lamp. In the first picture snapped, you can see the investigator standing in the area near the lamp with no sign of any activity—human or otherwise. Little did anyone know that the next picture would reveal one of the best images of a full-bodied apparition

In the next frame, the investigator now has two fully formed apparitions standing behind him.

we have ever been able to record with a digital camera!

The Mirror

Looking over the investigator's left shoulder, you will see the image of a full-bodied figure, complete with glasses, looking at the camera. On the right shoulder of the investigator, you can see the form of another

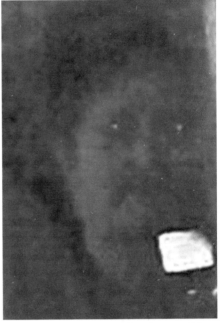

In this image, you can see the closeup of the full-bodied apparition looking over the left shoulder of the investigator.

spirit peering over his shoulder. Not one, but two ghosts chose that particular time to pose for the camera! The other image shows a closeup of the apparition that was seen in the mirror that night in the store. I can assure you that the image in the photograph bore no resemblance to anyone present at the investigation!

When I was shown the evidence from the investigation that included these photographs, my mind was convinced forever that our living world is inhabited by souls from the afterlife. Additionally, they are capable of appearing as they did in life, as full-bodied apparitions. I did not realize that the story of the apparition in the mirror had only just begun.

About six months later, I was out of town attending an antique show when a customer came into the store and purchased the mirror that was in the photograph of the apparition. When I returned from the show, my staff mentioned the sale of the mirror, but I did not give it much thought. At the time, I did not realize that there could be a strong spirit attachment to a possession valued in life. Several months elapsed and I was once again reminded of the mirror!

The customers who had purchased it came back into the store and started to talk about how they had suffered some really bad luck. Their house had burned down and resulted in an almost total loss of their personal items along with the structure. It seems as though the firemen answered the call and thought they had succeeded in putting out the fire. After they left, the fire restarted and their house burned to the ground, destroying everything that was inside.

As my customer told the story, they mentioned that they had hung the mirror close to an exterior door. When the firemen first came to the house, in an effort to save some of the personal items, they carried out the mirror that had been purchased at Golden Lane. When the house burned to the ground, it was one of the few possessions salvaged from the disaster! Could it be that spiritual intervention resulted in the mirror being saved? All I know is that the mirror that had clearly reflected the apparition now exists in its new home and all of the other possessions were destroyed. I believe that the mirror still has a spirit attachment that will continue to protect the item.

The Ring

When dealing with the paranormal world, truth can indeed be stranger than fiction. A couple of months later, I was witness to another example of a haunted personal possession. We were participating in an antique show in Texas, when a jeweler friend of mine was attempting to sell a diamond horseshoe ring. (I believe this is also an example of the ghosts getting even.)

Since Connie and I had become involved with the paranormal, my friend had taken great pleasure in making fun of our beliefs in the spirit world. One morning, a couple of days before the ring incident, we arrived to find a ghost made out of a sheet in the

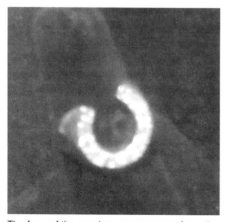

corner of our booth. There was also a pink doll to remind us of our child ghost, Clarissa, a permanent resident at our store. Until this time, everyone in our area of the show was having a good laugh at our expense.

As the show progressed, a young lady was interested in purchasing the ring for her boyfriend. She took a picture of it with her cell phone and intended to send it to him for his approval. When she examined the photo, there was the clear image of a man's face in the center of the ring. My friend called me over to look at the picture. I voiced my opinion that it was a spirit attachment and the prior owner wasn't quite ready to give up his ring. Needless to say, the young lady lost interest in

The face of the previous owner peers from the diamond horseshoe ring in this example of a haunted personal possession.

purchasing the ring when she realized that the spirit of the prior owner was still attached to it. The incident also marked the end of ghost jokes taking place at our expense. Since the ring event, my friend has actually participated in our paranormal sessions and has received a message from a deceased friend. The spirits really do act in mysterious ways.

The results of multiple professional investigations, photographs of a spirit presence and subsequent events, created the evidence of a spiritual presence that would forever alter my life. My conversion to an unquenchable belief in the spirit world is now complete. As I look back on the events of the past several years, I find myself on an incredible journey and this book is but a part of another chapter in the learning experience.

Tips for Using an EMF Meter

Spirits are energy that can emit an electromagnetic field. When a spirit is present, its energy fluctuation can often be detected by an EMF meter. The following tips will be helpful:

• Many spirits are rapidly moving. Their presence will not always show up on the meter.
• Stationary or slow-moving spirits will often indicate a fluctuation in energy levels readable on the meter.
• It is important to understand the background electromagnetic readings in the area being investigated. Wiring in the walls, or lighting, can give off energy that will be reflected by the meter. Make sure you do not mistake background readings for paranormal activity.
• Lights can affect EMF readings. It is a good practice to turn off overhead lights as they can often create a false reading.
• A ghost can communicate with the investigator by moving close to the meter and intentionally creating a spike in the energy level.
• The K2 meter is an EMF indicator with lights that come on indicating an increase in electromagnetic fluctuation. Spirits can be asked to answer questions by making the meter blink once for "yes" and twice for "no."
• EMF meters are a good indicator if an item, such as an oil painting or ring, has a spirit attachment.
• Heavenly Guides do not give off energy that can be detected on an EMF meter. Energy emission is a characteristic of earthbound spirits.

Chapter 2

Owning a Haunted Business

The building that currently houses Golden Lane Antique Gallery dates back to 1877 when it was first opened as a shoe factory. Today, it is a 30,000-square-foot facility holding antiques and fine art. When you look at the early pictures of the shoe manufacturing process, it becomes obvious that the operation was a sweat shop typical of this period of the Industrial Revolution. Small children would have been required to work on the crude equipment in areas that could not be reached by adults. Safety guards and protection gear were unheard of. While I have no written records of incidents within the store, I am sure many individuals were injured or possibly killed as a result of working there.

Beatrice

Spirits also follow favorite belongings. As you walk through the store, it becomes obvious there are thousands of items on display in the Gallery. At Golden Lane we are aware of multiple items that are haunted with a spirit presence. There is one large oil painting of a woman in a black dress from the Baltimore area that has a strong spirit presence. We have had several clairvoyants tell us that the spirit's name is Beatrice and she is a very unhappy soul. One evening, I watched as a guest was physically pushed from behind while standing in front of the oil painting. There was no one anywhere near her to have physically moved her. The clairvoyants also tell us that she hates to be called "Bea." We've had multiple female responses over the Ghost Box when we have tried to communicate with her spirit.

Joseph

There is another oil painting in the store with a strong-willed spirit associated with it. Our first encounter came well over a year ago, when Barbara Lee, our clairvoyant, was informed that the name of the spirit was Joseph and he did not like the music we were playing on our public address system. Since that time, he has made his presence felt in

Oil paintings can have a strong spirit attachment. His name is Joseph and he has a strong personality.

In this picture of a residual haunting, the barrel of a ghost cannon can be seen above the real cannon.

many different ways. When customers bring dogs into the store, they will often begin to shake and pick up their ears for no apparent reason when near the portrait. Animals seem to be much more aware of a spirit presence than humans.

The other day, a very sensitive customer came into the store and immediately commented about our large spirit population. As soon as the lady came through the door, she became dizzy and felt heaviness. I introduced myself and offered to show her around the store. Whenever a person comes into Golden Lane, I am very careful not to mention our spirit locations to them. My goal is to see if they really are sensitive to our local ghosts.

My tour started by leading her past the booth where the oil painting of Joseph hung on the wall. I watched her reaction as she walked by the booth; it was as if her body was suddenly pulled toward the picture. She spoke in a loud voice, almost yelling: "Stop pulling my arm." The spirit had actually exerted a physical force on her arm, trying to get her to come into the booth. There was no question that this customer possessed a well-honed ability to communicate with the spirit world, and the spirit world wanted to communicate with her. Joseph, in particular, seemed very anxious to have a conversation with the customer.

Several months later, I was standing at the front of the store and a customer asked me if I would accompany her. She advised that a painting was talking to her and she wanted to buy it. She took me directly to the portrait of Joseph. She explained that she was sensitive and that the man in the picture asked her to take him home with her. In this case, the image really *was* talking to her! Joseph now resides in a new home and I am certain he is very happy.

Residual and Intelligent Hauntings

A residual haunting is a playback of a past event. An intelligent haunting involves a spiritual entity interacting with the living world.

Perhaps the best example of a residual haunting is my picture of a ghost cannon taken on the Gettysburg Battlefield, in Pennsylvania, at the scene of Pickett's Charge (see image on page 15). Note the barrel of the ghost gun above the real cannon. During the charge, Union guns were lined up hub to hub in this exact spot and their thunderous fire left a ghostly imprint.

During a recent professional investigation at Golden Lane, there was the recorded sound of a work buzzer calling the employees of the past back to their work stations. The sound of a door, long removed, being slammed was also heard on the tape when it was reviewed after the investigation. Apparently, there is a residual energy that continues long after the real event.

One night, we were holding a mixer for the local Chamber of Commerce. As about ten of us were standing around the food table, there was suddenly a rumbling sound, like a piece of equipment being moved across the floor overhead. Everyone in the room heard the unusual sound. I thought my store manager was upstairs moving a piece of furniture, but I decided to investigate, just in case there was a problem.

When I walked up the stairs to the upper level, the door to the second floor was closed. I opened it and saw that the lights were out and there was no possibility of a living person finding their way in the pitch-black area! What everyone in the room heard was the sound of a residual haunting, probably the moving of equipment, from when the building was a shoe-making facility. As we were cleaning up later in the evening, my employees heard the sound again from the secured upper level of the store. There were a lot of witnesses to the spirit activity on that particular night.

Armed Intruder, or Not!

Perhaps one of the more amazing stories of an intelligent haunting happened on a cold February night in 2008. It had snowed the night before and, as a result of the lousy weather, we had a quiet day at the store. After locking the store and setting the alarm system, I drove to a local restaurant and started to order dinner. Just as I was sitting down, the alarm company called and informed me that the intrusion alarm went off at a rear basement door. She would dispatch the police as I rushed back to Golden Lane.

Upon the arrival of the police, we carefully made our way through the store, especially inspecting the rear door that the dispatcher had said caused the alarm. Our flashlights showed that the door was tightly closed and we had probably suffered a false alarm.

We went back to the front of the building, re-set the alarm system, and locked the front door. I apologized to the officer for the false alarm and returned to finish my dinner.

As I was preparing to pay my dinner bill, the cell phone rang again. It was once again the alarm company telling me the system indicated an intruder had opened the same back door. She had dispatched the police one more time. I informed her I would once again meet the officer at the store. I made a mental note to have the alarm company fix the system in the morning.

We have a very good local police force and the same responding officer drove up in a far better mood than I would have shown under the circumstances. As we unlocked the door I uttered a few cuss words concerning how our evening was being disturbed by the faulty alarm system. As we walked down the steps to the lower level and opened the interior doors, I could feel a rush of cold air on my face. Maybe someone had really broken in to the store! As we cautiously approached the door, we could see that one side was wide open leading to the outside. The door had been tightly closed and secured less than an hour ago when this same officer and I had inspected it.

The officer, with his hand on his gun, slowly walked to the door with his flashlight and lit up the snow around the area of the entrance. To our amazement, there were absolutely no footprints in the fresh snow around the area of the open door! Whoever or whatever opened the door had left no trace in the snow! At this point, I didn't know if we should call for backup or an Exorcist.

As I could see the look of total puzzlement on the officer's face, I figured it was time to mention the existence of our spirit residents. My exact words were: "I know you are going to think I am crazy, but this building is haunted."

His reply was not exactly what I anticipated. He said: "I grew up in a haunted house and this kind of thing used to take place where we lived. Let's get out of here."

At least he didn't think I was crazy. We locked the door, re-set the alarm system, and left the building. Since that time, we have not had an issue with that back door. I guess our residents proved their point: they could get our attention whenever they wanted.

One afternoon, I was working on a remodeling project preparing the room where we would be holding our paranormal sessions. I was putting up hardware to hold the curtains that would surround the perimeter of the room. In the center, I had placed a flat top table where the items for the project were carefully arranged. At this point of the project, I was using an electric drill to place the brackets that would hold the rods. Just as I finished hanging one, I heard the sound of something metal landing at my feet. This bracket had been lying on a flat table five feet away from where I was working! It was also the next item I required in my project! My spirit friends were trying to help me finish our room, so we could begin our sessions. They have indeed been very cooperative in our supernatural experiences.

A Flying Book

In October 2011, we had a mother and teenage son register to attend one of our paranormal sessions. When I talked to her on the phone, she explained that her mother had recently passed and she hoped we could make contact with her on the Ghost Box. I replied that we would be happy to try, but that there were no guarantees and the successes of our sessions lie in the hands of the spirits.

The mother and son arrived during the afternoon and introduced themselves. They had arrived early and wanted to check out the building and shop for a few antiques. I went back to my office and they left to explore the store. A little later, they came up to the front desk carrying a book in their hand. There was quite a story tied to it.

While they were walking by the booth of our antique bookseller, the book came off the top shelf of the display and landed at the son's feet. When they looked at the book, it was *Little House on the Prairie*. The mother said it was her favorite book as a child and that she wanted to buy the book. Apparently, the spirits were helping our sales force.

That evening, we began our paranormal session with the mother and son in attendance. It was obvious that an orb was making its presence known. As we watched the screens that allowed us to observe the spirits in live time, an orb kept circling the couple. When we started the Ghost Box that evening, Barbara Lee heard the name "Ann" in her head. The guest replied: "That's my mother's name." Additional questions on the Ghost Box made it obvious that her deceased mother was present and had something to say.

I asked the spirit if she threw the book at her daughter. The answer surprised me as a clear "no" was heard by everyone in the room. The son immediately posed the question: "Grandmother, did you throw the book at me?" This time the answer was "yes." The young man asked another question: "Were you trying to get my attention?" Across the Ghost Box we all heard "yes." A final question: "Would you do it again?" "No" was heard by the participants. Our guests had an incredible encounter with their deceased family member. On this particular evening, we had a reporter from the *Gettysburg Times* present and this story was printed in their paper.

Lights

As you enter Golden Lane Antique Gallery and walk straight ahead, you will pass through a doorway into a large room. On your left, you will find a light switch that controls three large fluorescent lights on the ceiling of the room. This entranceway isle is also an area of very active spirit activities. I have several videos of the activity in this area, including orbs swarming a rocking horse and a small ectoplasm cloud moving in the area. We believe that this is the part of the store occupied by our child ghosts.

On several occasions, I have entered the store in the morning and found these three lights shining brightly. While there is always the possibility that we forgot to turn off the lights, they are in a prominent place and can hardly be missed when we lock the store and turn on the alarm.

One evening, another employee and I were in the process of shutting down the store. As I was sitting at the computer closing the day, I had a clear view as he threw the switch on the lights and the room turned dark. About this time, I looked out the window and saw a customer approaching the door. I walked to the door and told him that we were closed and would open at 10 a.m. the next day. As I turned and walked back to the computer, I looked to the right and realized that the lights that were recently turned off, were burning brightly again. My employee was sitting behind the counter and had not moved. No one *living* had gone anywhere near the light switch! As I turned off the lights, I asked the ghost kids if they would please leave them off and not run up my electric bill.

In the same area of the store we have a metal door that leads to a utility closet and a stairway that leads to a small unimproved basement area that is quite spiritually active. (When the *Living Dead Paranormal* group filmed their Internet show, they caught the clear image of a shadow figure in this basement.) The door has a lock on its knob that has to be pushed in and turned. There is almost no chance that it would be pushed in by accident. Since the closet is used multiple times a day, we never bother to lock it.

On many occasions, our employees have gone to the closet and found the door locked. Everyone has been instructed not to lock the door. We keep the key in the office and, as a result, whenever the door is locked, we have to make a special trip. One day, I was working on the lights in the store and needed supplies that were in the closet. On three different occasions I returned to the closet and found the door locked. Since I was the only one using it, I can assure you I was not the one locking the door. I suspect our children ghosts were having a good laugh at my expense.

One evening in November 2012, we were conducting a paranormal session in our viewing room. There are ghost cameras throughout the store, so we can monitor activity anywhere in the building. When I checked the lights on the upper level, the entire area was dark, indicating that everything was normal. As we were getting ready to end the session, I looked at the screen and noticed that a light had been turned on in the case room on the upper level. It is not uncommon to come into the building in the morning and find this light has been turned on by our spirit friends.

Not only can the spirits turn on the lights, they can also turn them off. At the end of the session, I escorted my guests to the front door and told my wife, Connie, that I would go upstairs and turn off the light. When I opened the door to the upper gallery, it was pitch dark. Not only had my spirit friends turned the light on, they also turned it off, knowing I would not leave the building wasting electricity. My guess is they were having a good laugh on the other side at my expense...again!

Running Children

Proof that the children were playing games with us came one day when a very sensitive customer opened the door to a large cabinet in the vicinity of the closet. I asked the customer if I could help her with the cabinet, thinking about the possibility of closing a sale. The customer replied that she was not interested in buying the cabinet, but that she was playing hide and seek with a child spirit. I asked her to see if it was the same spirit that kept locking our closet door. The customer replied that the child spirit was giggling. My suspicions were confirmed as to the culprits locking the closet door.

One night, as my wife and I were closing the store, I watched on the closed-circuit security cameras as she locked the upper level and turned out the lights. Connie came downstairs and we prepared to leave the store. As we were standing by the front desk,

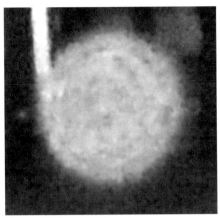

A blue orb was photographed in Golden Lane Antique Gallery. If you look closely, you can see the face of a woman in the orb.

we both heard the distinct sound of footsteps on the floor overhead. As she and I looked at each other, we realized that the spirits were moving around over our heads. This was not the first time we'd heard footsteps overhead, nor would it be the last.

If you are in the antique business, one of your biggest fears is an out-of-control child running through the store, breaking rare and valuable items. One day in September 2010, I was standing at the front desk with one of my employees. We looked up as the sound of a child running across the floor overhead was clearly heard by both of us. After uttering a few cuss words about parents not controlling their children, I ran (actually a fast walk) up the stairs to confront the parents and the child. As I entered the room where I had heard the footsteps, I realized that the room was empty. Figuring that the family was in another part of the building, I went through the entire upper level without finding anyone. I even went back and checked the security cameras. No living person had been on the second floor when we heard the sound of a child running across the floor!

Music

Apparently, our spirits in Golden Lane have strong opinions about what music we play over the public address system. One morning, I unlocked the door and as I entered heard music playing very loudly over the system. It was a different genre and the volume was much higher than we play during store hours. I am absolutely sure that the system was turned off when we closed the store the previous evening. I believe that our resident ghosts wanted to party overnight and needed some background music.

Lady and Orb

One morning I opened the store and flipped on the lights. While I am not overly sensitive, out of the corner of my eye, I clearly saw a woman in a white dress moving rapidly down the far aisle. This is the same area where I photographed a blue orb with the head of a woman in it as seen in the picture on this page I firmly believe that the woman I saw in the white dress that morning is the same spirit that can be seen in the blue orb.

My experience with all the paranormal happenings in our building here at Golden Lane Antique Gallery leads me to the conclusion that our store is one of the most haunted buildings in the country. When you unlock the door in the morning, you have no clue what bizarre experience will take place, but you can be quite confident that something will happen at the time you least expect it.

A Guide for Taking Better Paranormal Pictures

When I am photographing paranormal activity, I use a metal bar that holds three cameras. Since most people cannot see the spirit activity, you will need to take random pictures. On an average evening, I will shoot as many as 800 frames on the three cameras. The more frames you take, the better your chance to capture the activity. You will need multiple cameras. One of my three cameras has been modified for full-spectrum, infra-red through ultra violet wave length, photos.

- There are images that will show up on full-spectrum and not on regular cameras, and vice versa.
- The flash recovery time on a digital camera is too slow. Consider using multiple cameras mounted on a metal light bar. I use three cameras, one being full-spectrum. The activity may have ended by the time your camera has recovered to take another picture.
- When activity takes place, you need to take as many images as possible.
- Some makes of lenses are more effective than others. For example, my Canon camera does not record the details of paranormal activity as well as Kodak cameras.
- Spirits draw energy from camera batteries or cause cameras to malfunction. If one camera fails, you will have two for backup.
- Use a digital camera with enough capacity to enlarge small areas of the picture. Set your camera to the highest resolution possible. If you capture activity, it will probably only be a very small portion of your photograph that needs enlargement. High resolution will avoid the detail from being pixilated.
- The camera should have a clear back screen. I continuously watch the back screen to determine any activity taking place that cannot be seen with the human eye.
- All pictures should be reviewed on a large screen monitor. Paranormal activity can be quite difficult to recognize. Take a close look at high-energy orbs. Quite often they will have the face of the spirit in them.
- A good flash is required for all pictures, even those taken in daylight.
- The camera should be adjusted for an ISO of 1600. This will allow a higher speed shutter setting and still get suitable distance at night.
- The shutter speed should be set for 1/200 of a second. Spirit orbs move very rapidly and a fast setting is required for detail. Shooting with a fast lens speed might be the most important tip for paranormal photographers.

- Focus is a problem in paranormal photography. Auto focus should be avoided. A rapidly moving small object in the foreground will cause the background to be out of focus. I use a manual focus set at around 20 feet. Your paranormal image may be too small to be recognized by the auto focus.
- Carry sufficient batteries as backup. I have been forced to change batteries as many as four times in one evening.
- Do not attempt to take pictures in the rain or when there is ground fog. Water in the atmosphere will appear as orb shaped when you use your flash.
- If the orb in your photograph has a sharp edge, it is probably not a spirit. Look for a diffused or fuzzy edge.

Chapter 3

A Channeling Session in Salt Lake City

Our progression in communicating with the afterlife took a giant step forward when I was introduced to the technique of transcribing messages from a Spirit Board. Similar to an Ouija board, the Spirit Board is designed to protect the users from any messages that might come from the dark side. In our initial paranormal adventures, a Ghost Box allowed us to hear the actual voices of the ghosts. Unfortunately, our communication was restricted to short, difficult-to-hear phrases. On the Spirit Board, a person with clairvoyant abilities channels the spirit energy from the Heavenly guides to spell out the messages in detail. Once we mastered the board, our knowledge of the other side grew almost exponentially.

The story of how I was led to a group of individuals in Salt Lake City that would teach me the methodology of transcribing direct communications from the guides is told in the next chapter, It's Preordained. My goal in this chapter is to explain in detail the miracle of the Spirit Board and introduce the reader to the concept of Heavenly guides.

Spirit Guides

From the time of conception to the time of passing, everyone has Spirit Guides that teach and provide information to lead us through an incarnate life. There are personal and Master Guides. Master guides are on a higher plane and have the ability to predict the future. Most personal guides have been through the reincarnation process and have to increase their soul experiences to the point they help others. We have talked to Master Guides, whose feet have never touched the earth, as well as Saints who lived the holiest of lives. Everyone is born with the ability to communicate with personal guides, but as we grow older, our minds close and much of the abilities are lost.

You do not have to be clairvoyant to contact your guides, but you must learn to re-open your mind. As I was to find out, the guides help us to learn, and hopefully make the right decisions, as we move along our life path. I am going to let that information sink in for awhile. There will be a lot of information about Spirit Guides as we move along in this book.

Board Channeling

My introduction to board channeling came when I received an email from my friends in Utah, in 2009, letting me know that I had a Spirit Guide named Sterling that was using me as a writing portal. It took a little while to digest this information, but it did make sense that some kind of divine intervention was helping me publish a book dealing with the paranormal. Actually, as I think about it, there could be very little other explanation for my newfound writing skills, other than divine intervention.

This first spirit message from our friends out West gave me some insight into what was happening in my life. The idea that I had a Spirit Guide named Sterling who helped me create a book had sunk in and I was impatient to see what other information would be passed on by their Spirit Guides. Unfortunately, business kept me back East and I had to wait several months to get back to Utah.

The individuals in Salt Lake City who transcribed my message had no knowledge of my personal information, yet they were telling me things about my life and why events were taking place. For three generations, my friends at Ninth House Bookstore, located at 3443 South State Street in Salt Lake City, have been interpreting the messages of the Spirit Guides. Their father had designed a talking board like the one pictured here and they have been receiving messages on it for almost forty years. Having founded the Ray of Light Research Center, their research work concerning the metaphysical and spiritual dimension has gained worldwide recognition.

The Spirit Board used in Salt Lake City.

That fall I returned to the Salt Lake area and my friends invited me to attend a channeling session. I had no idea what was about to take place, but I was very anxious to find out.

As I entered the room, I realized the channeling messages were going to be transcribed from a special Spirit Board. The board consisted of a round glass top table with the letters of the alphabet and numbers around the outer edge, and the words "ok," "yes," "hi," and "no" on the face of the board. The entire face of the board was covered with glass. The planchet,

A clairvoyant uses the Spirit Board while a person acts as scribe and copies the messages of the Spirit Guides in Salt Lake City.

or pointer, was a large shot glass! The shot glass and board were cleaned and lubricated to make the shot glass move easily over the board.

Two of my friends took a seat at the table and the session began immediately, as though the guides were as impatient to give their messages as I was to hear them. The messages started as one of the individuals with his fingers on the shot glass began to call out letters that were, in turn, recorded by the scribes. As the first letters formed words, my jaw started to drop. I have printed the words of the guides exactly as recorded in bold type. The session started out with:

Hi Guys, Gooood to see u. Yes, we have a lot to say today.

The guide wasn't kidding about what was about to happen.

A month earlier, back in Pennsylvania at one of our sessions, a guest had asked if the spirits realized they were dead and not part of the living. Our Spirit Guide in Salt Lake City, without any prompting or prior knowledge, relayed the following message, one letter at a time, on the talking board:

Yes, first, we are not them, we are past life.
We know we are deceased, dead as a door nail.

That answer certainly seemed to be clear enough!

My clairvoyant friend in Pennsylvania, Barbara Lee, has been a huge source of information and inspiration concerning the paranormal and spiritual world. Deeply religious, she has spent much of her life helping living individuals and troubled spirits to find peace. Without her, the sessions at Golden Lane Antique Gallery would not be possible. If you have read any of my writings, she is often mentioned because of her incredible abilities. The individuals in Salt Lake have never met her and are not aware of her capabilities.

The following statement by the Spirit Guide should not have come as a surprise:

First, trust your lady, Barb; she is fantastic. She has it dialed in.

The spirits shared my opinion of Barbara Lee, two-thirds of a continent away. Apparently, good works really *are* noted by the spirit world. I made a mental note, or maybe the guide planted the thought in my head, that when I got back to Pennsylvania, I would construct a board and try it with Barbara Lee.

I have always considered myself a pretty good photographer. My book *Haunting and History of the Battle of Gettysburg* includes over 200 pictures of paranormal activity on the Gettysburg battlefield. Paranormal photography requires special techniques and I had been discussing with my associates how to take better pictures of spirit activities. The next answer from the guide seemed to come out of nowhere.

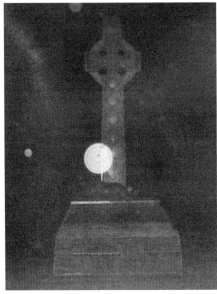

The Celtic Cross monument on the Gettysburg battlefield is lit by a large spirit orb.

Yes, you need a faster camera. Yes, you are dragging the image. Yes, Happy! The guides want to tell you more about you, and your tech support wants to get in how this works.

They were even using modern terminology! Since returning to Pennsylvania, I have followed the advice of the guides by increasing the shutter speeds while using the flash. As a result of the changes, I have been getting some amazing pictures. At times, I think the spirits actually pose for me.

In my first book, I discuss the negative things that have happened to me at the Celtic cross on the Gettysburg battlefield. This is the spot where the Irish Brigade suffered very heavy casualties. I have had spirits follow me and even throw a stone at my truck one evening at this location. When I went there with a clairvoyant, she told me that the spirits really didn't want me there. The next statement on the board helped clarify my reception at the Cross. The glass pointer spelled out:

The spirit of an artillery sergeant is seen by his gun near Devils Den on the Gettysburg battlefield.

As for you on the battlefield, those old Scots don't like no one.

At least I won't take it personally!

Next came another bit of information about a picture I had taken on the Gettysburg battlefield. It was an image from Smith's battery above Devil's Den. During the battle, the guns were captured by the Confederates with heavy Union losses. The message spelled out on the board was:

Animals have spirits, too. One evening, this ghost dog seemed to be posing for a picture.

The old sergeant in front of the cannon is really proud.

As you can see on the image above, there is the ghost of a soldier standing in front of the cannon. No one present in the room could have had any idea of the existence of this picture.

I have taken several pictures of ghost dogs on the Gettysburg battlefield and the same dog in multiple areas of the battlefield, many miles apart. On different occasions, I make the joke that I have a pet ghost dog that follows me around. The next message delivered on the Spirit Board made the joke seem not quite as funny. It was:

Yes, the dog follows you around.

At least I think the dog is friendly—it doesn't bite and you don't have to take it out for a walk.

The session was about to get very personal as the guide began to give me information about my prior life. At this stage of my paranormal education, I didn't know for sure that I'd had a prior life! They began with the following quote.

*Yes, first we want to address the soul named Barry.
Yes, his name is not Barry but Barnard. It is important
that Barry knows why he is Barry this life.*

Apparently, the guides help arrange similar names through a succession of incarnate lives.

The channeling statement that I found to be quite amazing was next to come from the guides.

The old lady in the rocker does not care; she ain't budging.

A Forgotten Incident

Up to this point, I had no problem understanding the messages that were being relayed by the scribes. This message made no sense to me at the time. We had never had an instance of an old lady in a rocker in the store. As I was rewriting the notes from the session the next morning, I suddenly realized the intent of the message.

Over a year ago, I had participated in an investigation of the Allenberry Playhouse in Boiling Springs, Pennsylvania, with other members of the P.E.E.R. paranormal investigative group. Midway through that investigation, Barbara Lee commented that there was an old lady in a rocking chair that wanted to talk to her. She described the old lady's appearance in detail and subsequently had a discussion with her. She was the deceased mother of the current owner and she was not pleased with some of the practices of her sons, namely not keeping fresh flowers in the Mansion house. I had completely forgotten the incident at the time of the channeling session in Salt Lake City.

The guides had commented on an incident that had completely slipped my mind. According to the guides, the old lady has no intention of passing over until the Playhouse was operating to her satisfaction. The spirits had commented on an incident over 2,000 miles from Salt Lake that had completely slipped my mind. I would have to rate that a "10" on the scale of amazing things.

The session lasted almost three hours as the scribe recorded various messages, all of them pertinent and to the point. Several of the messages will be covered in their own short stories. The session ended with the following message:

*Hey out there, turn it up, O.K. We are excited for you to
show this to Con and Barb. They will love it. Thank you and Boo!*

Not only did they know my nickname for my wife (Con), they had a great sense of humor. The guides were correct; they did love it! Additionally, I am "turning it up" by writing this book.

At the completion of the session, I was invited to try my hand at the Spirit Board. As I lightly placed a finger on the shot glass, it began to slowly move toward the letter "m" with no assistance from either myself or the clairvoyant. It spelled out the word "money" and then "goodbye." I guess the guides had run out of patience with me, but I hope the money part of the message comes true!

Before I left "my home" to go back East, I built my own talking board and took it back to use in our own paranormal sessions. As I anticipated, Barbara Lee was incredibly tuned in and a natural channel. The first evening we tried the board, the Spirit Guides cooperated by providing us with some unbelievable information. I have absolutely no doubt that the spirits had preordained the complex series of events that lead to my bringing the miracle of the talking board back to Pennsylvania. As you will see in the remaining stories, the Spirit Guides have provided access to information about the future, as well as helping our guests to reunite with deceased family members and friends. I truly believe there is no such thing as a "coincidence."

Using a Spirit Board

Author attempts spirit board for first time in Salt Lake City.

The spirit, or talking, board is a means of contacting and communicating with the spirits from the afterlife. The existence of a talking board dates back to the ancient Greek and Roman Empire. In China, boards similar to the Ouija were used to communicate with the dead. Native American tribes used a squdilatc board to obtain spiritual information and to locate lost objects and persons.

• The board consists of the letters of the alphabet, the numbers 0 through 9, and message words such as *Hello, goodbye, yes* and *no*.
• Best results come when a medium or an individual sensitive to spirit energy acts as the channel between the living and deceased.

- Since the pointer must move freely, the board should be covered by glass and the pointer must also be glass. A lubricant such as lemon oil should be applied to the glass. Free movement by the pointer is essential.
- It is always a good practice to record the session on a digital voice or video recorder.
- Prepare for the session by focusing mentally on the spirit presence with whom you would like to communicate. Include a request for their presence in your prayers.
- Always start with a prayer of protection from evil appearing during the session. Never seek evil or ask for it to appear. Negative energy is real and can be very unpleasant and harmful.
- The medium and another participant will lightly place their finger on the pointer. Care must be taken not to influence the movement of the glass.
- A scribe should record the letters as they are called out by the participant.
- Always test the Spirit Guide. Ask them specifically if they are of God. If they do not answer, take your fingers off the planchette (or glass) and end the session.
- Ask specific questions of the guide. Test them for information. If they don't answer the question, you may have asked for information that cannot be supplied.
- Try to have your questions prepared ahead of time. It becomes very difficult to think when overcome by the emotion of getting messages from deceased loved ones.
- At the end of the session, always thank the guide; tell them you appreciate the information they have provided.

I am repeating the following instruction because of its importance.
Never invite an evil entity to make its presence felt or appear on the board.

Chapter 4

It's Pre-ordained

My adventures with the paranormal have led me to conclude that one really has little control over much of life. It sometimes seems that major life patterns have been manipulated by powers much greater than our own. Since being introduced to the spirit world and looking back on the events that have shaped my life, I now realize that a huge number of the occurrences have definitely been the subject of divine and spiritual guidance.

As I review the events in my life that led to following my Karma path of enlightening individuals about life after life, it becomes apparent that forces beyond my control have been in play for a very long time. Life-altering events can be traced back over thirty-five years and beyond—actually, way beyond. During the late 1980s, my professional life was consumed by following my vocation in the construction aggregate and trucking business. Operations were conducted from an office building in the small town of New Oxford, Pennsylvania, known as the Antique Capital of Central Pennsylvania. (Incidentally, New Oxford is only eight miles from Gettysburg, the scene of an extensive spirit presence.)

Located across the street from our office was a huge abandoned warehouse. The old brick building dated back to the late 1870s, when it was used as a shoe factory. It had been abandoned since 1970, and was in a state of disrepair. At this time of my life, I had never even bought an antique and had no desire to do so. One day, my partner in the trucking business came to me and suggested we purchase the abandoned building and convert it into an antique gallery. He had investigated the purchase price and it could be bought very reasonably. At first, I thought the idea had absolutely no merit.

After much discussion, I agreed to the purchase as a real estate investment and have it remodeled into an antique mall. My one condition was that he would take care of all the construction and oversee the management of the business. This arrangement worked for quite a few years, but the time came when conditions changed and I purchased the ownership share from him, making me the sole owner of Golden Lane Antique Gallery. Until that time, I had absolutely no intention of participating in the management of the building and especially the sale of antiques. By 2005, my dreams of not participating in the direct management of the business were shattered on the rocks of reality. Whether

I liked it or not, the economic truth of a failing economy was going to make Golden Lane Antique Gallery the center of my working life.

Connie and I had been living in our home near Salt Lake City, Utah, since the early 2000s. I had been an absentee owner for our antique business since the buyout of my partner. As I became more interested in the business, she and I traveled around the country participating in Art and Antique shows. We left the daily running of the gallery up to local managers as I pursued my other interests, until the dwindling cash flow of the recession caught up with us.

It was only after I was forced to spend more time at the store that I paid attention to the paranormal activity that was taking place in the building. Without the failures of my managers and the economy, I would have never had the opportunity to become acquainted with the spirit world of Golden Lane.

Whenever we would come to New Oxford to visit the store, Connie and I would stay at the Chestnut Hall Bed and Breakfast, owned by Steve and Tina McNaughton. As we became friendly with the innkeepers, we learned that Steve was the head of the P.E.E.R paranormal group and an author of books on the spirit world. His group would perform the investigations at Golden Lane that would yield conclusive proof of the spirit presence. It is my belief that our becoming good friends with the local paranormal investigators may not have been a coincidence.

As my involvement with the spirit world increased, I became closely associated with my friend, Barbara Lee. She is a person of phenomenal psychic ability. Much of what I have been able to accomplish would not have been possible without her help and encouragement. The circumstances leading up to our meeting, as I look back, also seem to have been totally out of my control.

It was not until I spent more time in New Oxford and stayed at Chestnut Hall that I asked Steve to bring the P.E.E.R group into the store in an attempt to investigate the unusual occurrences. Coincidentally (or not!), Barbara Lee was the clairvoyant who worked with his group on the investigations. I first met her when I was invited to participate in one of them.

On the evening chosen to verify the spirit presence at the store, a large group of investigators showed up—around twenty in all. When we broke up into four groups of five, I just happened to be assigned to the group with Barbara Lee. This *might've* been a coincidence, but I firmly believe the guides had their hands in putting her with me in that group. We were also about to have one of the more memorable events I have ever witnessed in the paranormal world occur during that investigation.

Clarissa and the Pink Doll

We'd no sooner turned out the lights when Barbara Lee made contact with the spirit of a little girl. She said the child's name was Clarissa and she was singing a nursery rhyme. The clairvoyant actually sang along with the child spirit! At the end of the song, Barbara mentioned that the child ghost was talking about showing us her pink doll. The investigation was getting off to really a fast start, especially for someone who did not believe in ghosts!

Child ghosts still like their dolls. This is Clarissa's pink doll.

I was holding a K2 EMF meter in my hand and asked Clarissa if she would come close and make the meter blink for us. As soon as I asked the question, the meter recorded an unusual electromagnetic presence: the lights on the meter began to blink on and off rapidly. The spirit might be a child, but she had some strong energy!

I then asked Clarissa if she would make the K2 meter blink once for *yes*, and two times for *no*. She obliged by making the meter blink once, the code for *yes*. I next asked if she would lead us to her pink doll. Once again, the meter blinked one time. On that positive note, we set out across the floor of the store in total darkness. Our group came to the first aisle and I asked her if we should turn down the aisle. The meter blinked twice for *no*. When we came to the next aisle, I asked the same question. The meter once again blinked twice for *no*. As we came to the third aisle the question was answered with a single blink, *yes*.

We turned left down the aisle on the positive command. After walking about ten feet, we lost all contact with Clarissa. Barbara Lee could not contact her and I could get no response on the K2 meter. As we went back to our original position in the store, we were amazed by the interaction we had all just witnessed. Little did we know that the most surprising part of the story was about to unfold.

A short while elapsed and it became time to take a break in the investigation and compare notes with the other members of the group. I began to turn on the overhead lights, so no one would break a leg in the darkened building. Once done, I walked up the aisle toward where we had lost contact with Clarissa earlier in the evening. As I approached the spot, I glanced up and noticed a pink doll in the case on my left. The doll was within ten feet of where we could no longer contact the child spirit. Clarissa had led us through a darkened building, gave us three distinct commands to make specific turns, and led us over 150 feet to her pink doll! The doll is now on permanent display at the store.

Barbara Lee had been absolutely accurate in her mental contact with Clarissa. The child spirit really did want to show us her pink doll. Within the first hour of the investigation, I had been introduced to the clairvoyant that would alter my life and was

33

shown a spectacular paranormal event that showcased her supernatural abilities. As I look back on the happenings of that evening, I cannot help but think there may have been a lot of Heavenly manipulation.

Soldier Spirits

As I became more and more involved in the paranormal, I got to know and better appreciate the talents and abilities of Barbara Lee. She invited me to accompany her to the Gettysburg battlefield and take pictures of her encounters with the soldier spirits. On one of the trips, I photographed her in conversation with a Confederate soldier that actually turned out to be her relation. As the months passed, we became better friends and more involved with each other's spiritual adventures.

The spirit of a Confederate cavalry officer is photographed on the Gettysburg battlefield.

When strange things would happen to me on the battlefield, I would ask her to go along to help me clarify the events that were taking place. I had taken pictures of a Confederate officer, standing in the same place nine months apart. Without filling her in on any of the details, I took Barbara to the location to find out what was happening. While channeling with the Rebel officer in her mind, she got his name. He was a Confederate captain of cavalry named Reed. I researched his name and found out that the officer was not on the official death roster for the battle of Gettysburg. After doing research on the Internet, I located his gravesite in Abbeville, South Carolina. She had used her clairvoyant abilities to give irrefutable evidence of the existence and identity of the spirit.

Contacting Spirits

When I decided to have paranormal sessions at the store, Barbara Lee agreed to help me with them. As we experimented with different devices and electronic equipment, we had more and more success in contacting the spirits. Our first attempts at contacting the spirits were with a modified radio, commonly referred to as a Ghost Box. We produced some hard-to-believe results, but could not clearly receive detailed messages. It is very difficult to receive audio messages over three or four words. We needed a better way to communicate and, as I now realize, the spirits had been working for years to show me the way.

Several years earlier, my wife, Connie, was called for jury duty in Utah. Those who know my wife of forty-nine years realize that she never misses the opportunity to converse with anyone within earshot. At the store, we have even nicknamed her "Bubbles" because of her outgoing and bubbly personality. As the trial progressed, she became friendly with another woman on the jury. After the trial, we invited the woman and her husband over for dinner and have since become good friends.

Several years later my wife confided to her friend that I was writing a book on the paranormal. Her friend in turn admitted that she was in fact clairvoyant, but did not mention it because she did not want us to think she was nuts. Our friend now disclosed that her entire family was psychic. Her mother, Carol Green, had published a book about Spirit Guides and was famous worldwide as a medium. Her family had been conducting channeling sessions together for the last forty years in the Salt Lake area. She offered to get me a message at her next session. At that time, I had no idea what a channeling session was, but I thought a message from the other side seemed like a cool idea.

About a month after I went back to Pennsylvania, I received an email from our friend with the transcript of what transpired during their channeling session in Salt Lake. According to the Spirit Guide, in my prior life, I was a Confederate soldier who was killed soon after the Civil War. I had a friend in that prior life named "Sterling," who was helping me tell the story of the brave soldiers that died in the War Between the States. Sterling was using me as a writing portal!

Since childhood, I have been fascinated by the Civil War. Being a true romantic, my first date with Connie, over fifty years ago, was a trip to the Gettysburg battlefield. This first channeled message gave me some insight into what was happening in my life. The individuals in Salt Lake who had transcribed the message knew nothing about me personally. Things were starting to get really weird. There are 3 million people in the Salt Lake Valley and I was introduced to the four individuals capable of transcribing messages from the spirit world concerning the lives of persons 2,000 miles away from Utah.

Throughout my dubious academic career, I avoided anything to do with English or creative writing like the plague. I managed to get a business degree and a Civil Engineering license with as few literary courses as possible. To everyone's amazement, since getting involved with the paranormal, I published my first book, *Haunting and History of the Battle of Gettysburg*. While not as yet a Pulitzer Prize winner, anyone reading it seems to think it is fairly well written. Sometimes I surprise myself with what I, or maybe Sterling, writes. When my wife first started to proofread my book, she asked me where I copied some of the statements. I guess that was a compliment.

After receiving the message about Sterling, my curiosity was highly aroused. I was anxious to pursue the idea of receiving detailed messages from the other side. The opportunity came during July 2011, when I went home to Utah for a short vacation with my grandchildren. During this time, I was invited to attend a channeling session with my friends. I have transcribed the exact words of the message from the guides in the text that follows.

Without any prompting on my part, the guides explained my mission or Karma:

Yours, is simple. Twofold. You will tell the dead you know
they are still there and to introduce them to Heaven if they need
and to tell the living there is more to life. Yes, from that we
promise you will have what you need and more.

They were telling me that my role was to hold conversations, lectures, write books, and whatever else was needed to inform the living that there is indeed life after life. Our paranormal sessions at Golden Lane are dedicated to that purpose.

In the pursuit of following my Karma, I have already seen amazing things happen. For instance, as I was writing my first book, I had a payment of $3,000 that was due for the first installment to the publisher. The week before my payment was required, a customer came into the store and purchased a piece of artwork that amounted to $3,000. Later, I had a second payment that was due amounting to $6,000. The week before the payment was needed a customer came in to the gallery and bought a piece of artwork amounting to $5,700. Those funds were allocated towards payment for the book. The guides had said in Salt Lake City that they would provide what was needed and more. They wasted little time in living up to that promise.

The Guides Were Ready!

It soon became evident that I was being taught to use the Spirit Board in order to continue the process back East. When I first attempted to introduce Barbara to the talking board, my suggestion was not met with a lot of enthusiasm. She had heard stories of evil appearing and false messages being given from the dark side. I finally convinced her that a lot of spirits had gone to a lot of trouble to bring her and I and the Spirit Board together in Pennsylvania. With quite a bit of trepidation, the time finally came for us to attempt channeling messages from the other side by means of the board.

Apparently, the guides were ready and waiting for our attempt. We began the session with a prayer, asking that no evil would come forth and that the messages would come from the guides of Heaven. Almost immediately the glass pointer began to spell out coherent messages. Barbara Lee was an incredible channel and the messages were almost overwhelming.

We learned there would be messages from Heaven-bound and earthbound spirits. Among the Heaven-bound spirits, there would be personal guides assigned to each individual and there would be general guides that delivered messages from angels, minor gods, and the saints in Heaven. We would be given information concerning past lives, the present, and events that would take place in the future. All of this would not have been possible without an unbelievable course of events that had taken place during the time of our current lives.

As difficult as it may be to accept the course of events over a thirty-five-year period that shaped our present lives, I am going to suggest that life plans can actually transcend generations and centuries. In the next chapter, you will hear the story of Jeff Silverman.

As you will learn, Jeffery was a friend of mine in prior life during the 1860s and the Spirit Guides have given us Jeff's Karma that extends to promises made during the 1860s.

One evening, Barbara and I were conducting a private channeling session at her house. Connie was present and taking notes. The session began with the name "Roy" being spelled out by the glass pointer. He identified himself as a general guide, not one of the personal guides we had communicated with in the past. He started out by spelling:

Ask your questions.

For the next hour we were given rare insights into events that would take place in the future and alter many of our lives. As the predictions slowed, I made the statement that Barbara Lee and I were on an incredible journey to which the Spirit Guide replied:

Yes, you are.

I asked the question: "Why were Barbara and I brought together to hear and attempt to carry out the will of the Heavenly Guides?" His answer reinforced what I had already come to believe. The pointer spelled out the message:

It was preordained.

Amen.

Chapter 5

Meet My Guides

Until I was introduced to the Spirit Board in Salt Lake City, I had no idea that there were guides in Heaven that were assigned to help lead a soul through their life journey. As I found out, these guides attempt to communicate with us through Heavenly energy. Earthbound spirits, in contrast to the guides, use earthbound energy. Since most of our experiences are with earthbound ghosts, we find that the batteries go dead in cameras and recorders, and we are personally exhausted after our sessions. The spirits have borrowed our energy for their responses. We also find that our sessions with earthbound ghosts are more active on the full moon because energy is available. Another good time is after a thunderstorm.

For many of us, the advice of the guides is often ignored or not recognized. Based on our experiences, some guides are multipurpose and some are assigned for specific tasks. We were informed that there are personal and general Spirit Guides. A general guide is a guide for all. We have found that a general guide is of a higher ranking than those on a personal level. Whenever we get predictions of the future, we are in contact with a general guide.

One such guide that introduced himself on several occasions is Ed Dietz. He has acted as an aide in bringing us contact with our earthbound spirit requests. We have referred to him as a "gatekeeper."

One evening, when Barbara Lee and I were conducting a session on the Spirit Board, the name "Roberta" and "Apprentice" appeared. When we asked if she was a guide, she once again spelled out the word:

Apprentice.

I then asked if she was an apprentice guide and the pointer spelled out the word:

Yes.

The next message was even more amazing:

I am with Ed Dietz and he is the teacher.

My guess is that Spirit Guides are promoted, but have to spend a period of time with a general guide as the teacher. We have learned that whenever Ed Dietz makes an appearance, there is going to be some very interesting information that usually includes predictions of the future.

Another general guide that acts as a gatekeeper is "Raj." When we asked for personal details, the answer revealed that he was from India. He was the guide that assisted us in bringing forward our friend, Kathie, who had attended our sessions as a living guest in the past, but had passed over. (Her story is told in Chapter 21, "Death Has It's Perks.") Raj helped her to deliver her message with strength and force. After an hour of getting messages with the help of Raj, I thanked him for his help. His answer was :

You are most welcome.

Our experience shows that the guides have great manners and are quite appreciative of our thanks and respect.

As we became more adept at getting messages on the Spirit Board, we found out that we had the same guides, wherever we were physically located. Whether I am in Salt Lake City, Utah, or Gettysburg, Pennsylvania, the same guides are with me. Distance or location means absolutely nothing to the spirits on the other side. My friends in Salt Lake have received messages for me while I am back East. If the guides want a message delivered, it makes little difference if you are within 2,000 miles or not.

When I began spending more time in the Gettysburg area, I became fascinated with paranormal photography. My friends suggested that I publish a book. After laughing at the idea for many months, I decided to give it a try. The result was my first published book. All of a sudden, I somehow had succeeded in getting enough words on paper to satisfy a publisher. My wife and friends wondered how I had managed to put the words together in some semblance of readability. Connie even accused me of copying the works of others, something I had definitely considered doing in school to avoid failing writing courses. The answer to my sudden writing ability was not what I expected.

As I began working on the book, the words would come relatively easy. In the book I gave the historical narrative about areas of the Gettysburg battlefield and included actual paranormal photos from that area. Whenever I would need pictures from a particular area, it almost seemed like the ghosts of the soldiers would pose for me. It did seem a little strange that Confederate spirits were more cooperative than the Union ghosts. I guess once a Confederate, always a Confederate!

Whenever I was at a loss for words, I would say in a low voice, "Sterling, give me a hand here." After asking for help, the words would begin to flow and the segment would be completed. If you trust in your guides, help will usually arrive! As I look back, I should have probably included Sterling in the dedication.

Fun Guide

One evening in February 2012, at a channeling session in Salt Lake City, I was introduced to my "fun" guide. At that time of my life, I did not realize there was such a thing as a fun guide! What follows is a direct quote from the transcript of the session.

I am Paul. I am small and small is a good thing for me. Some would call me a wee one, not a Wii?

[Not only does my fun guide make jokes, he has modern technical knowledge.]

Paul is from the old country. You and I traveled to the Americas to be free. You a boy and me 200 years young. Before me, there were no wee ones in the Americas. I was the first. We wee ones hide things. We help and we make cookies. We are elfs. I am your fun guide.

My fun guide certainly covered a lot of ground in that statement. He is an elf from the old country (Paul did not say what country), he hides things, and makes cookies. With a resume like that, what else is there to say?

Several months later, in a channeling session at Golden Lane, the name "Paul" was spelled out on the board, indicating that he had a message. I asked if my fun guide was making an appearance and the answer was:

Yes.

The wee one had traveled from Salt Lake City and was making an appearance on the East Coast. He apparently had something to say. I asked if he had a message for me and the glass pointer spelled out the message:

Have more fun. Goodbye.

There was no way I could argue with that message—short and to the point.

On several occasions, Paul has made his presence felt on the board. The Spirit Board has the term "ha, ha, ha" on one side of it for the guides to use when they think something is humorous. When Paul signs in, the pointer first goes to the "ha, ha, ha" statement and then spells out a message for Barry. Knowing Paul, you never have any idea what is coming next! The wee one certainly has a lot of spirit energy and is always a welcome visitor.

Scott Arrives

In late February 2012, I was about to leave Utah and return to Pennsylvania. My friends conducted a final channeling session, using the new Spirit Board I had made to use back East. About half-way through the session, the guide asked my friend, Doc, to get up and let me use the board. This was my chance for on-the-job training.

As K, another friend participating in the session, and I put our fingers on the pointer, the guide moved the glass around the entire alphabet, as if to get the feel of things. Then the message began:

Your guide for this is Scott; he is who is in charge. It will not be this easy. But hang in there, as Scott gets better. Boo, rest.

He could have signed off without the "boo." Whenever they use the word "rest," it usually means they are changing guides. In this instance, Scott was taking over to practice with me on the board.

The session was about to take a turn for the bizarre. As the glass began to move across the board, the message began to take shape. It began:

Scott has tattoos; yes, one of a naked lady.

Of all the messages I was expecting, the realization that my guide in charge of the Spirit Board had a tattoo of a naked lady was not high on my list.

For the rest of the message to make sense, a little background is required. While I attended Lehigh University, I was a member of the Kappa Sigma Fraternity. As my grades can attest, our house was one of the better party houses on campus. There was a distinct possibility that traces of alcohol could be found at our parties. In addition, since Lehigh was never a football powerhouse, I can confess to a bit of jealousy toward my friends from Penn State, always boasting, with good reason, of the Nittany Lion's prowess. In retaliation, I have always cheered for anyone that opposed Penn State through the years. Unfortunately, that practice meant I cheered for a lot of losers.

At the end of the tattoo of a naked lady comment, Connie chimed in by asking Scott if he was a Kappa Sig. His answer was:

He is! He is! He likes to drink. Yes, that is why his arm reads, Mom. He wears glasses, yes and is bald! He is six feet tall.

Up to this point of the message, I was in good shape with the drinking, glasses, and baldness, especially the baldness. Then the pointer spelled out the stake to my heart:

He is a 1923 graduate of Penn State, so go back and practice. Are there any other questions?

The realization that my future on the Spirit Board would be up to a Penn State graduate with the tattoo of a naked lady and Mom on his arm sank in slowly. At this point, I did not know whether to laugh or cry. The decision was made for me as Connie broke out laughing; so I laughed with tears in my eyes. I am well familiar with Karma, but this is ridiculous!

Afterlife: What Really Happens on the Other Side

After I got back to Pennsylvania, Barbara Lee proved to be an amazing channel with almost no learning curve. Scott has appeared to us on several different occasions, just to let us know who is in control. In October 2012, we were conducting a channeling session and were getting messages from a lot of spirits that were just passing through and had no relation to our guests. I asked Scott if he could help direct our spirit traffic. His reply was there were a lot present, but he would try. The next message was from a deceased family member of one of our guests. My guide did exactly what I requested. As we progressed with our sessions, Scott has done an amazing job, even if he was a Penn State graduate. I have been afraid to ask if he has any other tattoos.

On several occasions, Barbara and I conducted private board sessions to receive messages that will affect how we conduct our plans for the future. I refer to these sessions as "checking our ghost mail." One evening in May, Barbara was feeling quite a bit of grief. A good friend had just passed suddenly and she felt his strong spirit presence. At first, we tried the Ghost Box and could hear a male voice calling her nickname, "Bree." It became obvious that her recently passed friend had a message for her. We decided to get out the Spirit Board and see if we could get a detailed message.

As we began, the glass pointer spelled out the name:

Troy.

It then spelled out the message:

I am the guide for deceased souls.

I must admit that, at a time like this, my mind was hoping it wasn't time to become a deceased soul. Barbara asked if her recently passed friend was present and the glass pointer spelled out the word:

Hold.

There was a slight delay before the pointer began to move again. Maybe there is a public address system over there where deceased souls are called to the podium. In any event, the next thing that happened was the glass pointer spelled out the name:

Shawn.

This was Barbara's recently departed friend's name. Shawn began the session by telling Barbara how "freaked out" he was when he realized that his soul was now on the other side of the life veil. Apparently, he was killed suddenly in an automobile accident, along with his dog, that was also with him on the other side. He went on to say that everything was now "OK" and that he was with his family members. For the next thirty minutes, he and Barbara discussed messages for living family members and talked about his new life on the other side. The glass pointer moved very rapidly and with strength, very unusual for a spirit that recently passed. Barbara promised she would pass on the messages, and the memorable session with her friend came to an end.

As the session ended, Barbara asked if Shawn could make a small silver cross hanging from her dining room light move as a final sign of his presence. As we all watched the cross, it began to move slowly. Her good friend was not going to leave her anytime soon. Troy, the guide for deceased souls, had done a good job in allowing Shawn to carry out some unfinished business.

General Guide Roy

One evening in April, we were again having a private channeling session at Barbara Lee's house. I started the session by asking if there were any Spirit Guides present. The glass spelled out the name:

Roy.

When I asked if he was a guide, the answer was:

General Spirit Guide; ask your questions.

For the next several hours, he answered questions about the future that included a prediction that Israel would attack Iran, that there will be a time of rioting in this country, there will be food shortages, and a three-week failure of electrical power from a disruption in the atmosphere. Another prediction was that the Pope would resign before his death and he would be followed by two more Popes who would serve terms of short duration. (If the reader would like to keep current with the predictions of the Spirit Guides, visit, www.spiritspredict.com, where updating of the predictions that have come true and those that are still outstanding are logged.)

As the session continued, it became apparent that we had a very special guide with us on this night. I asked if Roy had ever been on earth in a previous life. His answer was:

I have never touched the ground.

I then asked if there were any other messages. The response was:

Amid all the turmoil, be happy and you will suffer least.

Next, I inquired as to the source of the messages. His answer was not what we expected. He spelled out:

Each General Guide has a saint for a master. Mine is St. Thomas Aquinas. He is responsible for such messages.

The final question on this evening was if Roy had any more messages. His reply was:

Go in peace and be happy in the Lord.

It is not every day that you can receive a direct message from St. Thomas Aquinas.

I have referred to Carol Green's superb book, *You and Your Board of Guides* on several occasions. In her book, the question is asked: "How many guides do you have?" The answer is: "It differs from each. How many are needed are how many you have." The next question asked was: "How long does a guide stay with us." The reply: "As long as we are needed."

Augustine

As Barbara Lee and I progress in our experience communicating with the Heavenly Guides, it appears that we are given the guidance of spirits higher in the Heavenly pecking order. One evening, we asked for a general guide and "Augustine" appeared for us. His answers were quite detailed and very religious in nature. At the end of the session, I asked if we could request him for our next meeting and he said he would attempt to reappear. Sometimes, I am a little "thick," but on the way back to the apartment, Connie posed the question, "Do you think it could have been St. Augustine?" By then I'd realized that almost anything was possible.

At the next session, I requested Augustine and he immediately confirmed his presence. I asked whether we were getting messages from the famous 4th century Catholic saint. His reply was:

I am, yes.

Barbara Lee and I were indeed honored by the presence of the great Christian scholar. When I told him we were blessed to be talking to a saint and that he was a great teacher of the word of God, his reply was:

I am still teaching.

The answers that evening were deeply moving to all present in the room. I hope I am doing justice to his words in this book.

Ground Rules and Promotions

Since we have become acquainted with the Spirit Guides, the one overriding lesson we have become aware of is that the more we learn, the more there is to learn. We have also found that there is information that is not to be passed on to humans. One evening, we had a guide named Bartholomew and I asked who would be the next president. His reply was:

*I cannot at this time. Some things have to
follow their course and not be interfered with.*

There are apparently some very strong ground rules in Heaven.

At one of our recent "Lifting the Veil Sessions," we found out that an acquaintance in a prior life can become a Spirit Guide for the reincarnated soul of a friend. The clients on this particular evening had attended our channeling session before and the wife had been very successful in contacting a family member. Her husband had not been successful, so we put him on the board with Barbara Lee. Our guest's name was spelled out on the board indicating that the spirit had a message for him. Next to be spelled out was:

Romano....I was a soldier.

The guest did not recognize the name spelled out on the board. When we asked the spirit to provide the date when he knew our guest, the answer was:

1820.

My friend could be forgiven for not recognizing the name of an acquaintance from a prior life almost 200 years ago.

We found out that the spirit and my friend fought together for the Italian army in a conflict in Africa during a previous lifetime. (Our research shows that the Italian army did fight in a conflict in Africa during the 1820s.) The real surprise came when the spirit sent the message:

I was one of your guides when you were young.

This was the first time we had confirmation that a soul could be promoted to a Spirit Guide. Is it possible that this soul had learned the lessons of life so well that he could act as a guide for souls that had not as yet learned the lessons of God? I think it is also quite interesting to note that souls stick together through multiple life cycles.

Guides communicate with us in many ways. Often, it is the little voice in your mind telling you not to eat that last peanut butter cookie. It can be a lifesaving message preventing you from pulling out into traffic. Some individuals have the gift of communication with their guides through deep meditation.

We have been granted the gift of communicating directly and receiving detailed messages with the Spirit Guides by means of the Spirit Board. As we have gained experience with the board, we have found that there is always a guide that comes forward to help us gain a message that will help open peoples' hearts to the spiritual world around us. My belief is that as long as we use the Spirit Guides to promote love and cooperation in the world, they will stay with us as long as they are needed.

Contacting Your Spirit Guides

For the average individual, there are various ways to communicate with your Spirit Guides. In this book, I describe multiple messages from guides and historic figures that were received on a Spirit Board under the guidance of a gifted medium. The board provides the means for transcribing detailed messages. It is possible to converse with your personal guides through various techniques of mental concentration.

- In many instances, your guides will come to you in your dreams. Contact will often happen just before you fall into a deep sleep or in the half-conscious state as you wake up in the morning.
- You can be successful in making contact with your guides, but it will take patience and effort to achieve the required mental state. You must firmly believe in your mind that contact will be made. It can occur on the first effort or take weeks of practice, but it will happen.
- Do not be surprised if your guide is not in a human form. I read of one person whose guide was a talking beaver. The first time I made contact with my guide, a head floated in front of my mind's eye and it startled me to the extent that I snapped myself out of my trance state. I was very upset that when I'd finally made contact, I'd screwed it up.
- You can contact your guides by controlling your mental state through meditation. Choose a quiet and comfortable environment. It is critical that you have the ability to relax and not be interrupted. Have a pen and paper available to record any impressions or messages that you may receive.
- There are various aids to achieving the required focus or concentration. Some people will burn a white candle and focus on observing the flame.
- Always begin with a prayer of protection. Ask that you will be protected from evil and that only the presence of love and light appear. "The Lord's Prayer" is always a good choice.
- Be specific in your prayers. If you desire spiritual guidance for an issue in your life, ask for it. All prayers are heard. In many of our sessions, the guides have told the guests the exact content of their prayers.
- The mind's eye has the ability to visualize an image that is not seen through the human eye. It is often pictured as being in the middle of the forehead. Some people attempt to meditate by clearing their mind, relaxing the muscles, focusing on the area of their mind's eye and mentally inviting their guide to appear.

• As you begin your meditation, you must relax your entire body. Start by taking deep breaths and focus on relaxing every muscle of your body, starting with your head and working down every muscle, right to your toes.

• Imagine being bathed in a white or golden light. Remain focused and relaxed. Wait patiently for the appearance of the guide.

• In the event that you receive messages from your guides, thank them for their appearance. At the end of all our channeling sessions, I thank the guides for their help and they always respond with a message appreciation and generally end with the words "God bless."

• Patience is an extremely important character trait in making contact with your guides. Don't give up. It may take a week, or it may take a year, but it will happen.

Chapter 6

The Story of Jeffery Silverman

The orb of Jeffery Silverman makes his first appearance.

If I were to tell you that it is possible to feel a strong emotional bond with a spirit, the average person's next call would be to the local asylum. We have a very strong and determined spirit in the store named Jeff Silverman. I know the time will come for Jeff to pass over and I also know when that time comes, I will miss him. He has talked with us many times at Golden Lane Antique Gallery over the Ghost Box and has become a regular visitor to our channeling events. Over the last few years, he has given me my prior life history, even including my former name, Barnard Carter. When I do a lecture, I play a recording of him giving his last name in a loud, clear voice for an amazed audience. Good spirits are hard to find and he certainly ranks at the top of the list.

Jeff's story begins in the summer of 2009. We were having a lot of paranormal activity at the antique gallery and I would walk through our store after we turned out the lights and take pictures with the flash on the camera. When taking pictures, I am always looking at the back screen of the camera to determine if there is any activity out of the ordinary. When this picture was taken, you could clearly see a bright orb. As I was reviewing the pictures later that evening on the computer, I saw the large and well-defined orb in front of the rear corner booth, almost like it was trying to say "Hello."

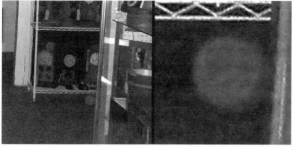

Jeff's face can be seen in the orb.

When I enlarged the photo, it looked like there was a smiling face in the orb. There had never been previous activity in this location of the store so my curiosity was now aroused. The next night, I went back to the same location with my camera and began to snap pictures. In my mind, I felt that there would be no additional activity in the same spot, since orbs move throughout the store with great speed and can be very difficult to photograph.

As I reviewed the photographs from the same area, there was a small orb in the same booth, under a book case that held a collection of small clocks. When I enlarged the orb, a distinct face became apparent. Looking closely, I could even see his dark hair. Whoever the Spirit, he certainly was trying to get my attention and he was succeeding. When we had conducted the professional investigations of the store in the past, there had been no

Jeff's face is seen as a reflection in the mirror.

significant action in this location. There was definitely spirit activity in the area now!

The next week I once again went back to the area with my camera. A huge mirror was in the back of the booth when I took the next set of photographs. A close look at the mirror revealed a very interesting reflection: the face of a man! I decided help would be required to find out the identity of the spirit.

An Investigation

Anxious to investigate the identity of the mystery guest, I contacted my friend from P.E.E.R., Steve McNaughton. My story of the spirit apparently posing for my camera also aroused Steve's curiosity. We decided to try the Ghost Box or paranormal voice enhancer and find out the identity of the mystery spirit. Ghost box technology had yielded excellent results in past investigations.

Along with Steve, his wife, Tina, and three other members of the paranormal group, the evening arrived when we planned to carry out the mini investigation. None of us realized this would be a night to remember. We set up a Sony video and audio camera as well as a digital recorder to assure the events of the evening would be recorded in detail. Steve started the session by asking the name of the spirit that was making his presence felt. The answer came over the Ghost Box for all to hear: "Jeff." Steve immediately asked if he was the spirit that was playing with me. The answer came back: "It was me." The session was getting off to a great start.

One of the investigators asked the question: Jeff, do you have a last name? In a deep male voice, much louder than the question, everyone in the room heard a voice clearly say: "Silverman." There was no doubt our spirit's name was Jeff Silverman and he was definitely introducing himself to our small group. If you have an interest in actually hearing Jeff's voice, I posted this video on my web site: www.ghostsofgoldenlane.com.

The next question asked by an investigator was: Jeff, why are you here? The answer that came over the Ghost Box was: "I made shoes." As mentioned earlier, the building that houses Golden Lane Antique dates back to 1877 when it was constructed as a shoe factory. It produced shoes under the name of Livingston Shoe Company until it closed in 1971. Jeff must have worked in the building when it was a shoe factory and was very proud of his vocation. We all looked at each other in amazement. So far, his answers were historically accurate.

At this point of the session, I asked Jeff if he knew Clarissa, the child ghost with the pink doll. His answer in a deep resounding voice was: "No," followed by the words: "I don't." Apparently, the afterlife is multi-dimensional. Even though the spirits are in the same building, Jeff and Clarissa had never met. On that note, we ended the Ghost Box session. It had indeed been a very memorable evening.

Talkative Jeff

Since that night, Jeffery has made his presence felt in many ways. One day, a lady customer came into the store who was very sensitive to the presence of spirits. She had never been in the store before and had no idea of the spirit activity that takes place in our building. I was talking to her in our lower level when she suddenly interrupted our conversation by saying there was a man standing in the corner of the room, saying his name is Jeffery. I simply said that he is one of our resident ghosts. Truer words were never spoken.

As I realized the extent of paranormal activity at Golden Lane Antique Gallery, we began to hold public sessions that would conclude with time being spent with the Ghost Box. Even on our worst evenings with the Ghost Box, when responses were weak and hard to hear, we could count on listening to Jeff give his name for our guests. We have even gathered additional personal information about his life. For instance, his wife's name is Beth and he lived in the town of Hanover, Pennsylvania, not New Oxford where the shoe factory was located.

In August 2011, a reporter from the local newspaper stopped by to write a story about the spirit activity of our store. It was about one in the afternoon and I took him downstairs to let him see our spirit viewing room. He asked me to show him how a Ghost Box works. I turned it on, explaining that quite often we can get a response from one of our resident ghosts. I voiced the question: "Jeff, are you here?" Above the background noise of the Ghost Box we heard a very clear: "Jeff." My next inquiry was: "Jeff, can you give the reporter your last name?" Across the voice box came a very clear and drawn out: "S-i-l-v-e-r-m-a-n," spoken slowly, so the reporter could get the name correct. The look on the reporter's face clearly indicated he had never interviewed a ghost before.

In Chapter 3: A Channeling Session in Salt Lake City, I related the messages that were given to me from the other side that concerned our operations in Pennsylvania. The most personal message that came from the session is this one, transcribed exactly as it was given to me.

Ask your buddy Silverman what U were known by.
Yes, he knows U very well because he has been waiting for
U to come back. Yes, he made a promise to U. Yes, after
this he can rest in peace and come home to be reborn.

I was stunned when I read this message the first time and I still am stunned whenever I re-read it. Not only did Jeff know me in my prior life, but he was sent here to fulfill a promise and has been waiting for me to come back—not to mention the fact that I somehow hold the key to him being able to rest in peace and be reborn. No pressure there! The total impact of all this is still sinking in. As time passed and our channeling abilities increased, I would learn a lot more about our agreement and my relationship with Jeff.

Not a TV Star Just Yet

In February 2012, we returned to our home in Utah for a short vacation. I also intended to pursue more knowledge concerning the spirit world by comparing notes with my channeling friends. My goal was to attempt to use my Ghost Box in conjunction with channeling sessions on the Spirit Board conducted by my clairvoyant friends.

One evening we were invited to their home, anxious to see if there were any messages from the Spirit Guides. After a very informative channeling session, it was finally time to break out the Ghost Box. As I adjusted the volume, I asked: "Is anyone present that would like to talk?" Over the background noise, we heard the reply: "Jeff." I asked: "Is it Jeff Silverman?" "Yes," could be heard by all. The spirit of Jeff Silverman had obviously traveled the 2,000 miles from New Oxford, Pennsylvania, to Salt Lake City, Utah. Additional replies left no doubt that Jeff was present in the room, a long way from our business back East.

After we got back to Golden Lane, Jeff continued to entertain our guests by conversing on the Ghost Box. We tried on several occasions to get a message from him on the talking board, but we received no reply. At least his responses continued over the Ghost Box.

In March 2012, the Arts and Entertainment Network approached us to provide information to appear on their *My Ghost Story* television show. Along with the photos of other activity in the store, I included the pictures and audios that had been generated by Jeff. On the day that I submitted the data, a couple of my friends, who are well aware of the paranormal, stopped by the store.

We were conducting some experiments to improve reception on the Ghost Box by using natural crystals, so I pulled it out in my office and turned it on. Our enhancements seemed to work, as we listened to some very clear responses. As we were getting ready to quit, I asked the question: "Jeff, are you here tonight?" We all heard a clear "yes" in response. My good spirit friend was present in my office and seemed strengthened by the use of the crystals.

I explained to my living friends a little bit of Jeff's history and that I had sent the information about him to California in an attempt to have his story included on *My Ghost Story*. The next thing I said to the Ghost Box was: "Jeff, I'm trying to get you on television." His response was: "Thank you." My ghost buddy even has great manners! Unfortunately, the release form for the A&E show required us to give them permission to fictionalize events. Since everything we do at our various sessions is true, I refused to sign their paperwork. Jeff will have to wait a little longer to appear on television.

Contact Methods for Jeff

As we continued to hold our paranormal sessions, I realized that Jeff was taking a less active role in our time on the Ghost Box. Weeks passed with no contact. With mixed emotions, Connie and I began to think that Jeff might have passed over as predicted by the Spirit Guides in Salt Lake City. It is inevitable that the time will come when we lose him, but as I mentioned before, it will be a truly sad event.

One evening in May 2012, Barbara Lee and I were conducting a channeling session on the Spirit Board. We had a small number of guests and we were all getting some personal contacts. I asked if anyone else would like to deliver a personal message. The glass pointer spelled out the name:

Jeff

I immediately responded: "Silverman?" As I watched the board, the pointer went to the word, "Yes." Jeff Silverman was still with us and had decided to make his first appearance on the Spirit Board and hopefully give us a detailed message.

As it sank into my thick head that my old spirit friend was back, my next question was: "Is everything okay?" He spelled out the word:

Sure.

I guess in a dimension that has no time, a spirit might not realize that it had been quite a while in earth time since we had last communicated. I did not want to miss this opportunity to let him know how we felt about his assistance, so I said: "You have been a big help to us here and I really appreciate it." The glass pointer spelled out the word:

Welcome.

My next question was: "Is there anything else?" He replied:

No.

My final thought was to tell him that I was finishing his story in my new book to which he answered:

O.K.

I guess this story will have to be his consolation prize for not appearing on the A&E network.

Jeff has become instrumental in showing guests at the store that orbs represent a true spirit presence. Our session room has special cameras that show the movement of orbs around the individuals in the room. I can usually ask Jeff to move slowly in front of the camera or pass over my outstretched hand so the guests can get a good look at him. The other day, his orb actually did two parallel loops, leaving no doubt that my spirit friend was appearing on command. The guests were amazed at his performance.

When we are communicating with spirits on the Ghost Box, responses are often weak and hard to hear. They actually have to learn how to communicate and the first attempt to talk on the box can be difficult. One night, we were having problems hearing a female spirit coming through. I asked Jeff if he could help the newcomer be heard on the box. His reply to my request was "sure." Then we heard him say: "You have to speak up." Incredibly, my spirit friend was instructing the lady how to be heard more clearly, just as I had requested!

As we finished the session, I told Jeff I was still working on the chapter about him and asked if he had read it. Once again, his answer was "sure." I then asked if he approved of it and he replied: "yes." My guess is he was probably putting the words in my head as I typed his chapter into the computer.

The Pendant

At our store, we lock the fine jewelry in a safe place every night. One morning, in October 2012, I was getting an opal pendant out of the tray and found that it was on the display board backwards. These photographs show the pendant as I found it on that morning and how it should be. When I closely examined it, I found that there was no swivel to connect the pendant to the bail. The chain had to be removed from the display

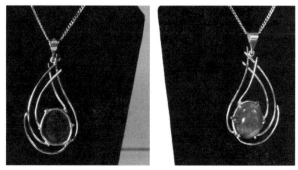

board to correct it for sale. I had put it in the lock box the night before and no one had touched it overnight. When I showed it to my staff, no one could figure out how the pendant could be reversed.

Left image shows pendant reversed on display. Right image shows proper display.

Later that month, I was putting the jewelry out for display and discovered that the pendant was once again reversed. Just to make sure I was not going totally crazy, I had my manager inspect the item and he agreed there was no way to correct the position of the pendant without removing the chain from the card. I came to the conclusion that I had to be getting help from my spirit friends.

Connie and I took the pendant into my office where the Ghost Box was on my desk. I turned it on and asked: "Okay guys, who is messing with me?" No sooner had I asked the question, than we heard the reply: "It was me." My suspicions were correct: I was getting some ghostly help. I already suspected what the answer was going to be, but I asked the question anyway: "Who just said, 'It was me'?" We heard a clear reply: "Jeff." My old friend must have known I needed some cheering up after the election results and decided to play a trick on me. How he ever managed to accomplish it is beyond my wildest imagination.

Hello, Hello

As we approached the holiday season, I once again wondered why my buddy, Jeff, was not showing up on the Ghost Box or on my cameras. Again, I began to think that my good spirit friend might have crossed over and I would not get to hear from him on this side of the life cycle. Little did I know that he would come back in an unforgettable flourish!

In late January 2013, I was preparing for a channeling session by showing some photographs to a woman and her husband in my office. This was the first session for the guests, but I knew she had some sensitivity to the spirit life. She was looking over my shoulder as I operated the computer keyboard. The guest suddenly stated that it felt like there was a hand on her butt! Both my hands were on the keyboard, so I knew I was innocent of any possible transgression. Her husband was also innocent. Strange things happen at Golden Lane, but this was really pushing the envelope.

Battlefield Soldiers

That evening, we had a very informative session with messages from major guides. As we continued with our personal contacts for the guests, I inquired if there were any more messages for anyone in the room. The pointer spelled out the name: "Jeff." My old prior-life friend was back!

I asked all the guests to say hello to Jeff. The response back was:

Hello, Barn.

He was still using my prior life nickname, short for Barnard. He went on to say:

Been awhile. Did you notice I haven't been around?
I had a mission to take care of.

He had truly been missed. I never thought to ask him what mission he had taken care of, and knowing Jeff, he probably would not have answered anyway.

My guest asked if I thought Jeff would know who put a hand on her butt earlier in the evening. I asked the question and the reply was:

Meant no harm.

Jeff Silverman was the mystery "gooser"! I didn't know whether to laugh or cry. Everyone else in the room broke out laughing, though, so I joined in. I made the statement that Jeff was one cool guy. His modest answer was:

So I have been told.

I finished the segment by telling the spirit that I considered him a good friend. His reply was:

...and I the same.

Jeff's spirit seemed to be in talkative mood, so I figured it would be a good time to ask some personal questions. I started off by asking if we had fought in the Civil War and received an immediate answer:

Yes.

Next I inquired as to where our regiment was from. The answer was:

Georgia.

We had been soldiers in the Army of the Confederacy. No wonder the Union Iron Brigade ghosts at the Celtic Cross monument were so unfriendly.

Having grown up in the Harrisburg area, I had always been drawn to the Gettysburg battlefield. As a child, my parents took me there on weekends. I now asked if we had fought at Gettysburg. Jeff's reply was:

Yes, that is why you are drawn here.

My prior life was definitely coming back to "haunt" me, so to speak.

Next, I asked if we had fought the first day. His reply was:

No, 2nd and 3rd day.

Being fairly familiar with the conflict that changed our history, I asked if we had fought in Pickett's Charge. His answer was:

No, Culp's Hill.

Culp's Hill was the scene of extremely fierce fighting for two days as the Confederates attempted to roll up the right flank of the Union Army, suffering heavy casualties. My follow-up question inquired if we were wounded and the answer was:

No.

At least we were not one of the 52,000 men that were killed, wounded, or captured during the three days of fighting.

Last year, I was photographing the battlefield after dark at the base of Culp's Hill in Spangler's Meadow. There is a heavily wooded path that runs behind a stone wall to Rock Creek. This was an area of intense fighting, and the Rebel soldiers were positioned behind the stone wall. It is also an area of heavy spirit activity, especially near the creek where they would have taken the wounded and dying. On that particular night, as I started down the trail, I was suddenly overcome with fear and a voice in my head said: "Don't." As I retreated from the trail and went back on the road, a tree fell on the trail in the exact location where I would have been taking pictures. This was a classic example of divine intervention or the protection of a guardian angel.

I now asked Jeff if he had been the one that saved my life on that evening last year. His answer was:

The fellows did.

I quickly asked if we had fought behind the stone wall in Spangler's Meadow and his answer was:

Yes.

Apparently, fallen comrades from my prior life had intervened to save mine on that night last year. Another one of my life mysteries had been solved. I am glad the tree didn't fall in Yankee territory; the outcome would have probably been much different.

The Agreement

In April of 2013, Jeffery made another appearance at our channeling session. I had been told two years earlier that we had made a contract concerning my current incarnate lifetime. I took this opportunity to ask him to explain the agreement. His first answer was:

Chapter 6: The Story of Jeffery Silverman

You agreed to participate.

When asked what I'd agreed to participate in, his reply was:

In what you are now doing.

With answers like that, Jeff could have been an attorney. The next question inquired whether he was satisfied with what I had accomplished so far. His message was:

Oh yes! We know you are doing your best.

I decided to get more information about our contract by asking if it was something we agreed to in prior life. His answer surprised me:

Not in prior life; before your return.

When I asked if we made the agreement while we were on the other side, his reply was:

Yes.

It never dawned on me that two spirits could make an agreement while on the other side! I can only guess what was in the fine print.

Since becoming involved with the spirit world, I've become aware that much of life is indeed preordained and part of a Karma path. My next inquiry was more of a statement than a question: "You are telling me that I actually had little control over my life." Jeff's answer was:

Kind of, sort of.

My suspicions were being verified and my next question put the icing on the cake: "So there could only be minor course corrections in my life." His reply was:

In a manner of speaking. Be happy. It's working out as we planned.

In my mind, I could see any possibility of retirement in this lifetime slipping away, so I asked: "Are you trying to tell me I am going to die here in Pennsylvania?" His answer confirmed my thought:

You bet! Yes, and remember an agreement is an agreement.

It appears that there is no wiggle room in a Heavenly agreement! I would also point out that the spirits view death in a much different manner than we do. For them, death is just the beginning to another life cycle. If I have learned anything about Jeff, he will probably try to talk me into another contract when I get over there, but, this time, I intend to understand the fine print.

As this book goes to the printer, Jeff is still present and helping us to explain the happenings in the spirit world. My current belief is that he will remain with us until our business here on earth is completed. As I mentioned before, in Salt Lake City, the guides informed me that Jeff made a promise in our prior life and that when it is fulfilled, he will move on to his next life. Jeff Silverman is the prime example of soulmates surviving through the millenniums. In the next chapter, Soulmates and Family Ties, the reader will get a better appreciation of the interrelationships between spirits and souls that endure for many generations. I now believe it is a distinct possibility that Jeff will hang around until Connie and I can move on to our next life together, soulmates forever. After all, to quote Jeff, "an agreement is an agreement."

Chapter 7

Soulmates and Family Ties

In order to understand the afterlife, there has to be an understanding of the relationships of the deceased souls to the living. When understanding finally comes, the intricacies of the relationship will often amaze. It took almost two years for this story to totally evolve, as we learned to communicate more efficiently with the Spirit Guides and the earthbound spirits that surround us every day. Reincarnation is one of the most difficult concepts to grasp. As you will see, it is a foundation belief to understanding the spiritual world that surrounds us.

Reincarnation

Reincarnation is when the soul or spirit returns to live in a new incarnate body. Some traditions even believe that the spirit can return as an animal, human, or maybe even a tree. I am not sure I agree with the animal or tree beliefs, but I am convinced beyond any doubt that the soul definitely returns to a new life, perhaps even hundreds of times. Each time the soul returns, it gains experience as it moves along its path to achieving some ultimate conclusion.

Many individuals find this a very difficult concept to understand or accept. I have addressed the idea of my soul returning in a different incarnate form previously in this book. There is much scientific evidence available on the subject. As I have evolved through the world of the paranormal, I have become a staunch believer in the reality of reincarnation.

I am also a firm believer in the concept of soulmates and family circles enduring through the generations. For many years, my wife and I have believed we were soulmates and meant to be together in this life. Can it be that our lives are actually preordained from the time of our birth? After reading this story, "reincarnation" and "soulmates" may have a slightly more important meaning.

Bert

In our initial experiences at Golden Lane Antique Gallery with the Ghost Box or paranormal voice enhancer, we would hear the names of various spirits being called out. On numerous occasions, we would hear the name "Bert" come over the box, but we were never able to learn much about him. Some of our ghosts, such as Jeff Silverman, are actually quite vocal and would provide information. In contrast to Jeff, all we could ever solicit from Bert was his name. We would ask questions on numerous occasions, but all we would hear would be a distinct: "Bert." His true identity remained a complete mystery.

One evening, Connie and I were conducting a Ghost Box session in a place and area other than our usual session room at the lower level. She mentioned that she had a very cold feeling on her back and legs. This can be a sign that a spirit is in close proximity. (We have recorded temperature drops of as much as ten degrees during investigations.)

One of our guests that night, who happened to be quite sensitive, told her, "That's because there is a man standing behind you." I handed the box to Connie and suggested that she check it out. "Jeff, is that you?" she asked. A man's voice replied: "No." Next, she inquired: "Well, if you aren't Jeff, who are you; what is your name?" The spirit answered very clearly: "Bert." Connie then asked if he was her buddy and he replied: "Yes."

For the past several days, as we were attempting to leave the office at night, the computer would come on with no human help. Connie's next question was: "Bert, are you the one that has been turning on the computer at closing time?" Once again, his answer was: "Yes." This was the first time we'd had a message other than his name. Whoever this was, he was clearly attracted to my wife. I didn't know whether to be jealous or not. As for Connie, she was delighted to discover that I wasn't the only one in the family with a paranormal buddy.

As mentioned, at Golden Lane, we have special cameras throughout the store that show the actual movement of the spirits in live time on our large-screen televisions. As we sit in the paranormal session room on our lower level, we can watch the spirit interaction with anyone in the room. One night, we had heard Bert's name over the Ghost Box on several occasions. I had forgotten an item from the front office and asked Connie if she would get it for me. I jokingly said: "Bert, if you are here, you can go with Connie." To all our amazement, as she walked out of the room, we could see a large orb slowly following her on the television screen.

Another name that we would hear on various occasions was "Helen." It would always be relatively faint and hard to hear, almost as if it the voice of a child. We were never able to figure out whether there was a relationship with anyone in our various groups. The closest we ever came to solving the identity of the female voice was in thinking that it might be my wife's deceased distant aunt who had passed, but we came to the conclusion that the voice was not her aunt's. We could never get any definite answers over the Ghost Box. Helen has remained a mystery, despite multiple attempts to communicate with her.

As time passed and we conducted more and more paranormal sessions, Bert became a regular presence at our sessions, but only when Connie was present. One night, we watched on the special cameras as she turned off lights on the main floor of the store and an orb followed her, almost seeming like she should be tripping over him at times. Whoever Bert was in his incarnate life, it certainly appeared that he had a close relationship with my wife that persisted to this day. Whenever Connie inquired over the Ghost Box if Bert was present, you could count on a positive answer.

In February 2012, we went home to Utah for a short vacation. I took some of my ghost-hunting equipment along. (You never know when there might be a paranormal emergency.) One afternoon, a friend of Connie's asked if she could see how the Ghost Box worked. Not wanting to miss an opportunity, I broke out the box as rapidly as possible. The three of us listened closely to hear if anyone attempted to make their presence known. I asked, "Is anyone present that would like to speak?" Once again, we heard: "Bert" come over the background noise. He had traveled over 2,000 miles to Utah with us—or I should say with Connie! I couldn't help but wonder if he also had a place in our bedroom.

The Quartz Pendulum

Another instrument that we have begun to use to communicate with the spirit world is the Quartz Pendulum. You can often get the pendulum to move in different directions, answering *yes* and *no* questions. One afternoon in Utah, Connie and I got out the pendulum and attempted to verify whether any spirits were present. As I held the pendulum in both hands, making sure not to influence its movement, I asked Bert to make the small piece of Quartz move toward Connie if he was present. In several seconds the pendulum was moving in a large arc and began to point directly at my wife. Whoever the spirit is that's following her, he is certainly not bashful in making his presence known!

The time came that I had to go back to the store in Pennsylvania. Connie remained in Utah and would fly back East to join me at a later date. As soon as I got back to the store, I decided to send her a small present, a quartz pendulum of her own. When it arrived a week later she called me to thank me for the present. It wasn't quite as good as a piece of jewelry, but you can't communicate with the spirits through a pair of earrings.

About an hour later, the phone rang as she excitedly explained the details of a session she had with Bert using the pendulum. Connie had made up a paper with a "yes" and "no" section for the pendulum, so there wouldn't be any misunderstanding as to the answers. Apparently he was a lot more talkative with me 2,000 miles away. I listened with amazement as she told me of her private session.

After a few preliminary questions that established his identity, she asked Bert if he was related to her in a previous life. The pendulum swung to the "yes" area of the paper. Using a process of elimination, she asked if he was her brother in a past life. Once again the answer was "yes"! Bert and Connie, or whatever her name was in her previous life, were brother and sister! I am not sure how I would have handled the answer if they had been husband and wife! No wonder he follows her around wherever she goes.

She then asked him if she was his little sister. Again the answer was "yes." Throwing caution to the wind, she then asked if she was "a pain in the ass little sister." At that point the pendulum swung to its highest point in an energetic affirmative answer. I have no comment to make over this answer.

With the questions about previous family ties out of the way, she asked Bert if he knew me in his previous lifetime. His answer was "yes." He and I had been friends in some past lifetime. I also knew his prior-life sister, who just happened to be my wife in this lifetime. I had always believed that soulmates remained together during multiple lifetimes. Connie and I have always felt a strong bond and we have referred to ourselves as soulmates for more years than I care to count. Here was verification from Bert, our spirit friend and also probable soulmate, that we had known each other in another time. In my research, I have come to believe that soulmates can be married in one lifetime and brother and sister in another. In the case of Connie and me, we learned that we were just acquaintances in prior life.

While Connie was using her pendulum in Utah, Barbara Lee and I were experimenting with the channeling board in New Oxford. The messages that came to us one evening in March revealed a lot about the events that had been taking place over the past year.

We had an active evening on the board with Barbara Lee's grandfather providing family information to her for the better part of thirty minutes. As he said goodbye to us, we asked if anyone else was present and wanted to communicate a message. The pointer went to the letters:

Helen.

Neither Barbara Lee nor I could identify the spirit attempting to give us a message. We asked if she was a guide. In response the pointer went to the word:

No.

We were dealing with an earthbound ghost.

I then asked for whom the message was intended. As we watched, the pointer spelled out:

Barry.

It was clearly my turn in the paranormal barrel! The pointer now spelled out the word:

School.

I attended Lehigh University, which was a school for men only at the time. Before that, I attended a medium-sized high school and, before that, a small one-room school in rural Pennsylvania with only thirty students. The name of Helen still escaped me. I asked to clarify whether I knew her in school and the answer was:

Yes.

The Ginkgo tea that I drink to improve my memory was definitely letting me down when I attempted to place Helen in my past. With my mind working overtime to put a face to the name, I asked Helen to spell her last name. In response the pointer spelled out the name:

Connely.

Her name was Helen Connely and I still could not place a face to the name. Next she spelled out:

3rd Grade.

Still, I had no clue. Now the pointer spelled out:

I was sick much of the time.

...and after a hesitation:

I passed on.

Helen was giving us a lot of information, but none of it was ringing a bell. Little did I know that a huge bell was about to be rung! Her next message was

You were a friend of my brother, Bert.

The implications of that statement were huge! After getting over the shock related to that answer, I asked the question: "Is this the Bert that is Connie's prior life brother?" The answer was:

Yes.

The next question was: "Is Bert here?" Her reply was:

Bert is not here; I am Helen.

Afterlife: What Really Happens on the Other Side

That was a stupid question on my part; I knew he was with Connie in Utah. Now I really asked the obvious: "Helen, were you Connie's sister in her prior life?" The pointer rapidly moved to:

Yes.

This gave new meaning to the term "distant relative."

My next question was: "Does this mean we were all together in a prior life?" The answer was an emphatic:

Oh, yes.

Trying to get more details, I asked what year Helen passed in her prior life. The glass pointer went to:

1840s.

At least I had a valid reason for not remembering her name. She had passed 170 years ago!

Recap: Previous channeling sessions on the Spirit Board in Salt Lake City had given me some clues about my prior life. I knew that I had been a Confederate soldier and had passed shortly after the Civil War. Jeff Silverman, our resident ghost at the store ,was a prior-life friend, but I knew little detail, since up to this time, we had never conversed on the Spirit Board.

Here was a golden opportunity to learn about my activities of 170 years ago. My next question was about the town in which we all lived. The pointer spelled out the word:

Oregon.

I asked if that was a town. Next came the answer:

No, Oregon Trail, follow.

I asked Helen if she had passed while on the Oregon Trail and her answer was:

No.

Then she said:

We left Oregon and separated.

My next question was: "Why did you separate?" We were taken back by her next answer:

Parents killed, Indians.

I asked if she was taken prisoner and Helen answered:

No.

She said they were adopted by other families. It was the custom in the early West that orphan families would be split up and adopted by other pioneer families. Apparently, Connie's prior life family was separated at an early age.

Still curious about the details of my demise, I asked Helen if she knew the site of my previous life's grave site. She spelled out the word:

Wyoming.

I then asked my age at the time of passing and Helen answered:

45.

That was a ripe old age in the pioneer West. This information actually confirmed my earlier sessions. If I had been born in the 1820s and survived forty-five years, my passing would have taken place just after the Civil War. Many of the Confederate veterans went West after the war, rather than face life in the decimated South. Many found their way to Wyoming. The pieces of the puzzle on my prior life were coming together.

With that, I told Helen that I would tell Connie that I had a conversation with her prior-life sister. The pointer spelled out:

You are most welcome.

Our amazing Spirit Board session came to an end with Bert and Connie's sister, Helen.

The next morning, I relayed the revelations of the past evening to my wife who was still in Utah. I asked her to take her pendulum and ask Bert if they had a sister named Helen. As I expected, the pendulum swung strongly to affirm the question. Apparently, the soulmates from the Oregon Trail—Helen, Bert, Jeff, Connie, and Barry—are still intertwined.

Since that time, Helen has reappeared with messages on the Spirit Board on several occasions. One evening she appeared when Connie and I were trying the board without Barbara Lee being present. When we asked Helen if she had a message, the pointer spelled out:

I love you.

Strong emotions run deep, even after 170 years.

We have tried on various occasions to channel with Bert on the board, but he has refused to communicate using that medium. He is fine with the pendulum or Ghost Box, but wants no part of the Spirit Board. Any time we ask him if he will participate with the channeling, the answer will be a strong "no" on the pendulum. The other evening, Helen let us know she was present during a channeling session. I asked if Bert was there and she answered:

He is off visiting.

It seems that Bert gets out of town when we have our channeling sessions.

From that first time in 2011, Connie and Bert have communicated on a regular basis with her pendulum. We ask him for advice and he generally is quite a help with making

decisions. On evenings when I plan to take paranormal pictures on the battlefield, we generally ask him if I should go or not. Whenever he says to go, I am usually rewarded with an outstanding picture. One day in July 2012, Connie received a strong "yes" that I should take pictures on the battlefield that night. The wingspan of the figure shown is well over twelve inches, so don't try to tell me it is a bug. Yes, I do believe in fairies!

Bert is with us every day and is continually making his presence felt. Some customers came into the store the other

A fairy is photographed on the Gettysburg battlefield.

day and started a conversation about our paranormal tours. It turned out that the customer was actually a film producer and was gathering information for a movie concerning ghosts in an insane asylum. His purpose for coming into the store was to purchase props for the movie. The more we talked, the more interested he became in our spirit friends.

He was looking for a place to bring the actors in the movie to gain experience with ghost hunting. I tried to explain to him that we do not have to hunt for our ghosts, they are with us all the time and we can pretty much communicate with them whenever we want. This concept did not exactly fit in with the way the paranormal is portrayed in the movies. My initial thoughts concerning their presence in the store was less than enthusiastic. He went on to explain that in this movie, the spirits would actually be portrayed with positive actions. With that comment, I began to pay a little more attention.

My next statement caught the film producer by surprise. I told him I would go into my office and ask them if they wanted the actors in the building. When he asked who "they" were, I explained that I wanted to check with the spirits themselves. We would get the Ghost Box out and ask them directly. Needless to say, he really wasn't expecting that turn of events!

He asked his son to come along into the office. I think he felt the need for a witness. When the box was working, I asked if either Jeff or Bert were present. Both the producer and his son heard a clear: "Bert." I tried to explain that we were talking to my wife's prior-life brother from the 1840s. The look on the producer's face said it all.

I got right to the point and asked Bert if he minded if I let them come in for a ghost hunt. His reply was: "What's that?" My ghost friend was not admitting to knowing about a ghost hunt. I tried to clarify by saying that they wanted to come into the store and try to find the spirits. The logic of trying to hunt for a spirit that was already present seemed to be confusing Bert. It was time to rephrase the question.

If you don't mind him bringing in his friends to look for you guys, please say "yes." A very clear "yeah" was now heard by all. Bert is never one to do exactly what you ask of him, but I assumed the "yeah" was actually "yes." I told the producer that he had the permission of the spirits to bring his actor friends into the store. He was also told that if the answer had been "no," they would not have been allowed to come in. The reality that the producer had just been interviewed by a ghost took a little time to sink in.

We have learned that Bert has an incredible sense of humor and is quite capable of playing jokes on his sister. The next chapter, Who Passed the Gas?, takes a practical joke to a new level. He continues to make us very aware of his presence and Connie and I feel a strong bond with the spirit. We have no doubts that reincarnation is alive and well!

Using a Pendulum

A pendulum is probably the easiest way to communicate with a spirit presence. The downside of using a pendulum is that you cannot achieve the detailed answers available with another spiritual device, such as a spirit board. An advantage of this technique is that a medium or clairvoyant is not required. A pendulum is a great starting point to explore your personal psychic abilities.

- In preparation for use, mentally pray that no evil comes through and that your spirit will provide answers to your questions.
- Be aware that an evil entity can come through and intentionally give you bad answers. Test by asking if the spirit is of God. If you do not receive a definitive "yes" answer, stop the session immediately.
- There are many types of pendulums. We use a simple quartz pendulum on a silver chain.
- When you receive your pendulum, cleanse it in salt water. Do not let anyone use your pendulum. This is one of your most personal items and it is only for your use.

- You do not have to spend a fortune on a pendulum. Check out eBay to get an idea of what is available and approximate costs. Spending more will not assure better results.
- Hold the chain between the thumbs and fore fingers of both hands. Make sure you hold your hand still, so you do not influence the movement of the pendulum. Be aware that your breath can move the pendulum.
- Until you become more experienced at using a pendulum, make sure your questions can be answered by "yes" or "no" and are simply stated.
- Keep your code for answers simple. We use a forward and back motion similar to nodding your head as "yes." When we thank our spirits for answers, they will make the pendulum swing in a circular motion that means: "You're welcome."
- When the pendulum moves sideways, like a negative nod of the head, the answer is "no."
- There are charts available for more complex answers that have individual numbers and letters. Another option is making up a chart to fit your individual needs. Just remember that the more complex you make the chart, the more you open the possibility for bad answers. You are dealing with spirits, not human beings.
- Use a recording device to keep track of the messages. Both your hands will be holding the pendulum so you will not be able to keep notes.
- At the end of the session, thank your spirit for its help.
- Remember that this is a single tool for communicating with the other side. The answers may not always be correct. If the answer directs you to do something harmful, stop the session and ignore the advice. A good spirit will never direct you to do anything harmful to yourself or another individual.

Chapter 8

Who Passed the Gas?

As we get to know our resident spirits, they become like old friends. In many respects, they show the same characteristics as humans, except they don't have bodies or the ability to communicate with us directly. As we have found out from experience, some of our spirit guests have a wonderful sense of humor. One night, in the middle of May 2012, we all found out just how good a sense of humor one of our regulars, Bert, possessed. A word of warning for the reader: if you are offended reading about certain human bodily functions, such as passing gas, you might want to skip to the next chapter.

In order to understand the story, I need to "pass" on some background information. Keep in mind that our friends consider my wife the sane one in our family. She is very considerate of other people's feelings and has been referred to as the saint in our marriage. Even my children have doubts about the sanity of yours truly, especially since I began writing about this paranormal stuff.

One morning, as we were in the process of opening our store, a customer arrived. In this economy, the arrival of any customer is a notable event. Connie was sitting in our office checking her email and I was in the lobby area putting the jewelry into a case. The customer was in the front of the store, but in a location that Connie could not see from her chair in the office. All of a sudden the quiet of the morning was shattered by the sound of a world-class passing of intestinal gas by our customer from the far corner of the room. (That was a polite way of describing the almost indescribable fart!) It even reverberated into the office where Connie was working.

For some unimaginable reason she apparently blamed me for the sound of gas being released in the lobby. The sound waves had hardly cleared the area as she rapidly rose to her feet, headed toward where I was working in the lobby, and said in a loud voice directed at me, "I heard that clear in the office." Fearing from experience that there would be more incriminating words to follow, I started to make as many hand gestures as possible in an attempt to save the customer on the other side of the case any further embarrassment. I knew he had heard every word she had just spoken concerning his gaseous explosion. I was also looking for an opportunity to plead my case of innocence. As Connie realized what she had done, there was the sound of a gasp and she hastily retreated back to the office.

Not wishing to make matters any worse, I choked back my comments until the customer moved out of the area and earshot. As the customer disappeared from sight, I could no longer hold back my emotions and broke out laughing at her embarrassment. As soon as I could speak, I told her that she deserved to have to checkout the customer and look into his eyes knowing he had heard what she said about his recent contribution to air pollution. Fortunately for her, she got lucky and the customer left without buying anything. It never occurred to me that Bert was watching from the other side and must have been laughing at his sister's predicament.

That evening we were having a paranormal session with several guests. Barbara Lee was present and actively contributing to the proceedings. We were trying to communicate with the spirits over the Ghost Box. It was a very busy night with multiple spirits saying their names and short messages, many trying to speak at the same time. As I listened to the responses from our earthbound spirits, I heard a strange sound for the first time in such a session. It was amazingly similar to the sound heard earlier in the day in the lobby of the store, just not as loud. Sometimes, discretion is the greatest part of valor so I kept my mouth shut. If it was an indiscretion on the part of one of the guests, I would pretend it never happened.

As the sound level of the responses on the Ghost Box lowered, I heard the familiar noise again. This time the sound was louder than the first. I looked around the room and noticed that everyone else was looking around the room. There was no doubt that our guests also heard it and were looking for the culprit. I decided to take the bull by the horns and asked the question as delicately as possible: "Did anyone else hear a strange sound on the Ghost Box." I then made the obvious statement: "It sounded like a fart." It was déjà vu all over again. With my experience from earlier in the day, I was certainly qualified to recognize the sound!

Barbara Lee is a very dignified and proper person. The sound of a spirit passing gas, loudly and distinctly, during our paranormal session did not meet with her approval. She exclaimed: "You stop that. It's not nice; get out of here." The offending spirit quickly made the sound one more time, apparently showing which side was really in control. At this point, there was nothing to do but laugh at the events that had just taken place. The laughter must have had the desired effect, as that was the last time we heard the sound that evening.

A series of words came over the Ghost Box that led us to believe that the spirits had a detailed message for the group that would be better transmitted on our Spirit Board. Barbara and I set up the board so we could communicate in detail with the other side. I could not resist the temptation so I asked the question: "Who farted over the Ghost Box." The glass pointer began to spell out the name:

Chapter 8: Who Passed the Gas?

Paul.

You heard me talk about Paul in other chapters of this book; he is my personal fun guide. The pointer now went to the message:

ha, ha, ha.

Paul thought it was funny, too. I then asked the question if he had made the noise. The pointer spelled out the word:

No.

Paul had obviously observed the entire scene, and being my fun guide, was not about to miss out in the festivities. He did think it was quite humorous, but was not the culprit. The identity of the mystery farter continued to deepen.

The next morning we opened the store as usual. After things quieted down, I started to tell my manager, Mark, the story of hearing the sound of farting on the Ghost Box. I usually tell him about the more bizarre happenings and this story certainly qualified. He also sees firsthand many of the unexplained occurrences that take place in the store and had seen Connie communicate with Bert, using the pendulum. In addition, Mark had also been present the previous day for the gas explosion. His comment concerning the situation made a lot of sense. He said: "Maybe Bert is making fun of Connie for what she said yesterday morning." As I thought about it, he may have solved the mystery.

I called Connie into the office where we would not be disturbed and told her about Mark's theory. She had seen other instances of Bert's sense of humor and agreed that there was a good possibility we could assign guilt for the transgressions of the prior evening to him. I asked her to get out her trusty pendulum and ask Bert if he was making sounds on the Ghost Box.

Connie got the quartz pendulum and held it steady. She took a deep breath and asked the question, "Bert, did you fart over the Ghost Box last night?" She barely got the words out as the pendulum began to move, slowly at first and then with growing momentum. It eventually moved so high, it almost hit her on the chin—a strong and definite "yes!" He was the culprit and proud of it! The brother from her prior life had found a way to make fun of her faux pas with the customer earlier that day.

At times like this, we always try to get confirmation by asking a question causing the pendulum to move in the opposite direction. I had Connie ask if Paul had made the sound on the Ghost Box. The pendulum slowed and then moved in the opposite direction. The answer was "no" to Paul making the sound. Bert had made the offending sound and was not going to let any other spirit take credit!

At this point, Connie and I were both laughing at the thought of him being able to play such an elaborate joke on her. We knew he had a good sense of humor, but this was incredible. Connie then said laughingly: "You really know how to pick on your sister; thanks a lot." The pendulum then began to move rapidly in a circular motion.

His answer was "You're welcome." There was no doubt that Bert bore the responsibility for the gaseous sounds. Hopefully, he got it out of his system (that was a joke).

Baked Beans in Heaven

A week later it was time for one of our regular paranormal sessions that featured a Ghost Box session. We had a couple of guests who had attended our channeling event before and brought their nine-year-old grandson along to see the ghost pictures that are part of my lecture. It was a full moon and the room was full of activity as we observed the spirits moving around the room on our large screen television sets. As I watched the action, there was no doubt in my mind that some of our guests from the other side were going to have messages on the Ghost Box.

True to my expectations, everyone in the room was having no trouble hearing the spirit responses over the background sound of the Ghost Box. Not only was the full moon beautiful to look at, it was providing energy for the spirits to use in answering our questions. Little did I know there were storm clouds, or maybe I should say gas clouds on the horizon. When I asked if anyone else had a message, we all heard the name "Bert." I should have known that when I heard the name come over the Ghost Box, there was a good chance that his sense of humor would result in our session taking a turn toward the dark side.

The responses on the box slowed as we could hear only background sound of the rapid scanning of the AM radio—apparently the lull before the storm. Suddenly, the quiet was broken by the sound of gas being passed. I quickly looked straight ahead without comment, sorting out the question of whether the sound came over the Ghost Box or from someone sitting at the table. I stole a glance at Barbara and I could see she was beginning to turn red. No doubt in her mind where the sound came from!

Once again, the sound came across the Ghost Box. This time our nine-year-old guest lit up like a Christmas tree. He knew exactly what he was hearing, just like on the playground at school. I blurted out the question: "Bert, did you do that?" A very clear "yes" could be heard over the sound of the scanner. Connie's ghost buddy was back and thoroughly enjoying himself. Barbara tried to save the day by telling Bert to stop it and that we don't do things like this. Her effort was rewarded by an even louder eruption. By now everyone in the room was laughing, especially the nine year old. I can only guess what he told his friends the next day.

In an effort to add a little more humor to the situation, I asked the question if they had baked beans in Heaven. Bert replied with a clear: "yes." Once again, the background noise was drowned out by laughter. I must admit that the image of a group of angels sitting around, eating baked beans, is not the way I envision the Heavenly experience. On that humorous note, we ended the session for the evening.

At the start of all our paranormal experiences at Golden Lane, our guests are told that we have no idea what direction the spirits will take us during our various encounters. On that evening, in particular, truer words were never spoken.

Tips for Using a Ghost Box

- There are commercial Ghost Boxes available for purchase. Make sure you check the scan rate.
- There are apps available for smart phones.
- If you make your own Ghost Box, information is available by searching "hack Ghost Box" on the Internet. Steve Hultay is a pioneer in hacking radios to make a Ghost Box and his website is most helpful.

Ghost Box.

  - Make sure the model radio you select can be hacked. Sangean has made changes to current models that make them impossible to hack.
  - The scan rate is very important, as the faster the radio scans the dial, the more you can be sure the word you hear is the voice of a spirit.
  - My Ghost Box scans the radio dial in 10 seconds, a very rapid scan rate. Any full word heard at that scan rate is a spirit. I only use the AM band as there are more stations available.

- When you start the session, make sure the spirit can answer with a single word. For instance, ask the spirit to start with: "Hello." A good follow-up if you hear the "Hello" is to ask his or her first name.
- Record all sessions with a high-quality recording device, preferably with quad sound. When I replay a session with earphones, I find that we have only heard approximately one-third of the responses in live time. You will also want proof of the replies by the ghosts when people say you are crazy.
- Get a good audio analysis program that will help reduce the background noise. You will hear more responses when you play back the recording.
- Vary the volume of the Ghost Box to find a level that is comfortable with the spirits. At times, I ask if I should increase the volume and they will often let you know what is comfortable.
- Do not expect long answers. They are not capable of more than a couple of words. It takes a lot of energy for them to answer.
- Address the spirits with respect and thank them for their answers. They will not cooperate if you insult them.
- If you are not getting responses, I usually ask if they would like me to end the session. Quite often they will say "goodbye" and you will know it is time to turn off the Ghost Box.

Chapter 9

There is More to Life

Quite often we see skeptics come to our paranormal sessions who refuse to believe in either the spirit world or the afterlife. Whatever the reason, these individuals seem to fear the concept that there will be an inevitable time to face what, to them, is the unknown. I have seen persons attend our sessions view spiritual presence in live time, hear the voices of earthbound ghosts on the Ghost Box, watch messages coming from the guides on the Spirit Board, and still refuse to open their minds to the existence of an afterlife. My guess is that only the act of dying will introduce them to the reality of the life after life.

My personal opinion is that when it comes time to face the inevitability of death, I would rather have some knowledge of what lies ahead. After listening to nonbelievers, I have no trouble understanding the fear an individual has of dying, if they believe death is like snuffing out a candle. There will be no one more surprised than an atheist about one minute after death. It should be a classic "oh, crap" moment. In my mind, death is the beginning of a new adventure, not just the end to a brief life on earth.

I have seen proof that there is more to life in many ways, but none more compelling than the results of channeling sessions on a talking board that took place in Salt Lake City in 2013. Many nonbelievers claim the messages delivered on a Spirit Board are fake and not to be believed. During the sessions, the letters come very rapidly and the words are totally in the hands of the spirits. Having participated in many hours on the Spirit Board, I can assure you there is absolutely no chance of being scammed by the clairvoyants with their hands on the pointer. The glass moves so fast that there are times when you cannot keep up taking notes. In our sessions at Golden Lane, we now give each of our guests the opportunity to put their finger on the pointer and participate in receiving the messages. Some of our most interesting messages have come with a guest on the glass pointer.

At this particular session, the Spirit Guides gave us a clear explanation of the difference between the spirits we talk to on the Ghost Box and the ones that communicate with us on the talking board. The messages that night explained profound information about the dimensions on the other side of the life veil. The following is an exact transcript of part of the session with the guides. Keep in mind these messages were spelled out one letter at a time on the Spirit Board:

We here are Heaven Bound. Your spirits are Life Bound. Life Bound means one has not given up the life energy. Heaven Bound means Heaven is your energy. Life Bound can come to Heaven but stay in life energy and Heaven Bound can visit life unseen but Heaven energy keeps them away from life.

The guide went on to further elaborate on the complicated workings of the spirit world:

Life-Bound spirits will not use Heaven energies. Heaven energy is like for angels and things. Most Heaven souls choose not to use earth energies. Your soul friends are different than guides. One is life energy and one is Heaven energy.

As I transcribed the words of the session, I realized just how much information was given in those few moments by the Spirit Guides. First of all, there really is a Heaven! This is going to really suck for a lot of skeptics and atheists. Not only is there a Heaven, it is a dynamic dimension inhabited by spiritual beings that manipulate events in the life plane using their own energy sources.

Spirit Guides are messengers from Heaven and rely on energy from Heaven. This energy apparently cannot be picked up on electronic equipment. There are no readings on our EMF (Electromagnetic Field) meters while channeling is taking place on a Spirit Board. Whenever we get channeled messages, the spirit presence does not show up on our special cameras that detect earthbound ghosts.

Let's examine the quote: "Your soul friends are different than guides." Connie and I are privileged to have a continuing relationship with earthbound spirits from our prior lives. In previous chapters I have related the story of her prior-life brother, Bert, and Jeffery Silverman, a prior-life associate of mine. The term "soul friends" reiterates the fact that soulmates exist and continue to influence current lives.

Spirit Guides communicate through channeling as opposed to earthbound spirits that can speak messages directly over the Ghost Box. We have never experienced responses from a Spirit Guide on a Ghost Box. They suggested in recent sessions that we use both the talking board and Ghost Box to communicate with the spirit world. It seems as though some of the earthbound spirits want to only talk on the Ghost Box.

In order for an earthbound spirit to communicate on the board, a guide is required to provide assistance. There are guides for deceased souls that help provide direct

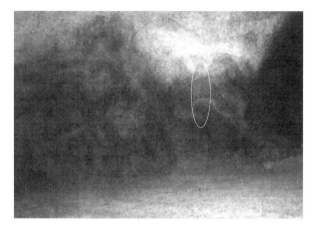

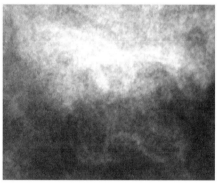

An angel on the battlefield. Note that the form of a soldier is in its arms.

communication on the board. The guide will tell us that there are several spirits waiting to come through and then a name is usually spelled out for the guest to recognize.

The spirits with whom we communicate on the Ghost Box are life bound and must draw on life-bound energies. This is why batteries go dead in the presence of life-bound spirits and EMF meters record their energy presence. It also explains why we are exhausted after a Ghost Box session, as the spirits use our personal energy to communicate. In many of the Spirit Board sessions, we do not feel the same drain of energy.

Life-bound spirits can pass from a presence on Earth to Heaven and back again, but must rely on life energy sources. In a previous Ghost Box session, I told my father, deceased for over forty years, that we thought he had passed over into Heaven. His response was that he had indeed passed over, yet we were talking to his spirit on the Earth plane. This was evidence that spirits could return from Heaven for missions on Earth.

Angels definitely exist! I already knew this from my photographs taken on the Gettysburg battlefield. Some clairvoyants have such acute powers that they can channel with angels. Barbara Lee works with Angel Guides who we found out are often the messengers of the saints.

One evening, I was photographing on the battlefield and snapped a picture that may actually be an image of a saint. As you can see on page 77, the form is seen in profile and seems to be in the superman position with its arms extended. I could not see the image when I took the picture.

There are Heavenly messengers other than the guides and angels. As we learned in other sessions, there is a hierarchy of minor gods and saints that act as messengers. I also suspect this category includes fairies and other elementals. One night, as I mentioned earlier, we had the presence of a General Guide and he stated he was delivering the messages of St. Thomas Aquinas.

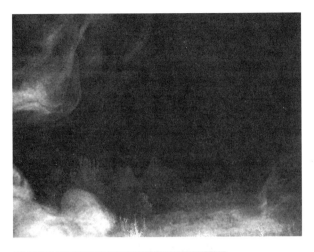

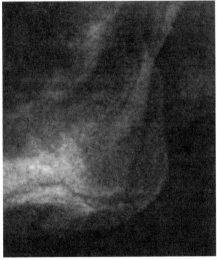

This angel is photographed in profile—possibly the form of a Saint.

In my previous channeling sessions, I had witnessed the fact that the information possessed by the Spirit Guides is all-knowing. They can supply little-known facts, completely unknown to the individuals using the Spirit Board. I had seen the guides refer to my wife by a childhood nickname known only to deceased family members and her parents, who were located over 2,000 miles from the channeling session. When Connie was small, her family referred to her as "Gerty" after cartoon character Gravel Gerty, because she often had messy hair like that character. The first time she ever attended a channeling session, the guide started off by spelling out: "Hello, Gerty." Needless to say, the greeting certainly got our attention!

As we have progressed in our abilities to use the Spirit Board, we have received predictions of the future. While the events do seem to happen, we have noticed that the predictions of time are not accurate. We believe this is due to the fact that there is no time dimension on the other side and they do not have a good handle on when the events happen.

In spite of all the amazing things I had seen in prior sessions, our Spirit Guides had topped themselves with the revelations given on this winter evening in Salt Lake City! They had paved the way to an understanding that would allow me to explain many of the spiritual happenings that were taking place around me.

The skeptics would approve of a final statement made by the Heavenly Guides on that evening in February:

Never believe anything you know is wrong. Question everything. Make them prove it. Yes, you will have scammers. Test on both sides, yes!

Advice in that final quote from the Spirit Guides sums up a philosophy that provides great direction for our daily lives.

A guideline that we have used in our interviews is to ask detailed questions that would only be known by the specific spirit. In our interview with Ulysses S. Grant, he was asked personal questions such as his nickname for his wife, Julia. He had referred to her as "the boss" since she insisted on handling the family money. To date, we have not been able to determine if any of the spirits were trying to scam us. (I wish I could say that about living individuals.)

The information given us on that winter evening was some of the most profound encountered to date. Whenever I give a lecture, I put the transcript of the statements concerning the earthbound and Heavenly guides on the television screen and read the words out loud in an attempt to explain the spirit hierarchy. In my mind there is no doubt that the guides provided sound information about what happens at the end of our current life journey. If individuals pay attention to this book, they may not have that "oh, crap" moment immediately upon passing from this life to the next.

Chapter 10
Predicting the Future

Since the beginning of time, humans have been attempting to predict future events. The ability to foretell future events is directly proportional to an individual's sensitivity to communicate with the Heavenly guides. It also depends on the guide's desire to pass on information to humans. There is certain information that they will refuse to divulge.

Our experience has shown that the General Guides have the ability to look into the future and accurately predict events that will take place. Since there is no time in their dimension, we have found that predictions as to when the event will take place are sometimes mistaken. For instance, we were told to expect Israel would attack Iran in June 2012. When I questioned the guide why it did not happen, I was informed that the plans were changed. The predictions generally come true, just not when you expect them to.

As I discussed before, there is a hierarchy of Spirit Guides that provide different types of information. A General or Master Guide is on a higher plane and delivers the messages of the saints or minor gods. These are the Heavenly spirits that will also answer questions about the future. General Guides have great knowledge and many have never had an incarnate body. Persons that have achieved spiritual greatness in life can become Master Guides capable of looking to the future. Our sessions have included visits from St. Augustine, St. Timothy, St. Thomas Aquinas, and St. Bartholomew. All visits by these spirits have revealed biblical history, as well as predictions of the future, many of which have proven accurate.

When a General Guide is present, all other spirit presence is blocked from the session. There is definitely a pecking order in Heaven. They will answer questions as long you do not cross the line and request information that is not for the betterment of all.

I asked my friends in Utah to check with their guides and attempt to verify some of the predictions we had received. I have come to realize that their guides seem to have a different personality than our local ones here on the East Coast. When asked about the opinions of the historical figures, the answer was:

Afterlife: What Really Happens on the Other Side

One soul's opinion is just that; you have to ask the General Guides and higher what their views are on the situation to understand more.

They also said:

Just because you are dead doesn't make you smart; they still have their own egos, agendas, and ideas.

I followed up by inquiring about the accuracy of the interviews with the historical figures:

Understanding this, what they are receiving is accurate and very fun and will make a great book or two.

Their guides agree that the historic interviews are accurate. I really like the part about a great book or two. When it comes to predictions, apparently we need to pay more attention to those made by the Master Guides than those of the earthbound souls. When we asked the question whether it was smart to get prepared, the answer was:

It's always smart to be prepared for the unseen and unknown. Everyone should have a little money buried outside in a safe place and a pair of clean knickers in their glove box.

If only half of the predictions come true, we are going to need more than a pair of clean knickers. I think this is where a couple of cases of MREs will come into play.

Our experiences also show that the guides will predict the future for common good, not personal enrichment. For instance, there is no way they will give you winning lottery numbers. They will also not give an indication of dire personal events. You will not get an answer to a question concerning your personal time of death. We have also learned that rephrasing a question will not lead to an answer. If they don't want to answer, you can rest assured there will be no answer.

Another area in which there will be no response is when the answer can have the effect of changing a preordained outcome. We asked repeatedly of various guides to predict who would win the presidential election of 2012. In all instances, they never gave us the outcome. The closest we ever came to an answer was that it would be a close election. They also predicted that there would be problems with the election. My guess is they may have been referring to the Internal Revenue scandal where certain groups were discriminated against that would have resulted in voter repression.

We *have* seen predictions of the imminent passing of a loved one. We had a guest one evening whose mother was in very poor health in a nursing home. The spirit of his aunt (his mother's sister and best friend) came through to let him know that his mom would soon be passing over and that his aunt would be there to assist her on her journey.

Not only had the guides brought a message of the imminent passing of the ill parent, but also a message was given that she would be assisted in her trip from the veil of life. Our guest left the session with mixed emotions. On the one hand, he felt grief on the pending passing of his mother, but he also had a feeling of comfort that the mother's inevitable journey would not be a lonely one.

Two days after the session, our guest called to update us on the condition of his mother. She had passed quietly in her sleep, as predicted two days earlier. He wanted us to know that they were very comforted to know that her sister had assisted with the passing. My guess is that his attendance at our channeling was preordained by his deceased family members to help bring closure to the passing.

As I became more involved with the spirit world, my Karma to tell others of the life after death became more apparent. I was given personal predictions that would ease my worries of the future. For instance, one of my first messages predicted a long life for Connie and me. In October of 2011, I received the message:

If you take care of each other, you both will live past 95.

While the assurance of long life is quite comforting, the thought of celebrating a 75th wedding anniversary is almost overwhelming. For my own personal well being, I am not going to pursue this line of thought.

One of my largest worries is how to pay our bills in this lousy economy. I am much too old to sit on a street corner with a tin cup. The art and antique business is dependent on discretionary spending and a lot of people's incomes are going toward filling gas tanks and putting food on the table—not a rosy economic picture. In addition, my pursuit of providing information concerning the spirit world takes a huge amount of time that could be diverted to generating personal income. The guides attempted to put my worries to rest with this prediction of the future:

For another maybe 4 years, the shop will keep you afloat.
When the books start to keep you afloat, you will
sell the place to some friends still to meet.

There is also a clear inference that I had better keep writing these books as rapidly as possible. Additionally, they gave me a pretty clear directive on our paranormal business:

Do you not see you can make more cash money expanding your
classes. At one time we discouraged people from gambling on the things
for income. It is just too hard to be income dependant on it, but
technology has caught up. Now you can expand out and make
great fun money doing the classes, worldwide.

My guess is that they have a complete business plan for me on the other side.

The predictions of the Spirit Guides do come true, sometimes very rapidly. One evening, we were channeling on the Spirit Board and the name of an ex-employee was spelled out for us. I inquired if the employee had passed and the letters spelled out:

Message, sick.

The next morning when I arrived at the store, I mentioned to my manager that we had received a strange message about the ex-employee. He inquired if I knew that the individual was sick with a very bad cancer. In this instance, the prediction had come true in less than twelve hours!

The Middle East

Since Barbara Lee and I have been using the Spirit Board, we have been getting dire predictions concerning the Middle East and the expectation of a major conflict. In May 2012, we were channeling and were told of imminent violence. We asked if there was any danger for the United States and the answer was:

A major assassination.

My follow-up question inquired as to the identity and the answer was:

Be a high figure.

On September 11, 2012, the dire prediction came true as our ambassador in Libya was assassinated by Muslim terrorists. This act of violence was also followed by massive riots. It definitely appears that the time of turmoil predicted by the Heavenly Guides is beginning.

Starting as early as March 2012, we have been receiving messages concerning an imminent war between Israel and Iran. The ever-changing conditions in the Middle East were reflected in the predictions of the guides. In March, the prediction was that the war would take place within a year of our time. By May the message changed to:

Be prepared for war.

Any day, Israel, US will now be involved.

When I asked if Israel would attack Iran, the reply was:

Both will attack.

With today's technology, I guess the odds are that the attacks will be simultaneous. We have been given predictions of war in the Middle East on five different occasions. Of course, a skeptic would say this prediction could have been made for the last 2,000 years.

On the same night that we received the prediction concerning the assassination, the next message was:

Expect WW3.

On that cheerful message, I inquired as to whether nuclear weapons would be used, to which the answer was:

Will attempt.

My follow-up was to ask if the attempt would be against the United States. The General Guide replied:

No, not at this time.

Next, I asked whether Iran will use nukes, to which the answer was:

They will try, as will North Korea.

My guess is the guides know more about who has nuclear weapons than our own defense department.

Barbara Lee asked if Jerusalem would be okay in the upcoming conflict. The answer was an emphatic:

No.

Next, we asked if Israel would be okay, to which the glass pointer spelled out:

At most, Israel will need help.

When asked if the United States will help, the ominous answer was:

Not the main support.

When asked who the main support would come from, the answer was:

France, Italy, and England.

The guides also said that Egypt and Syria would get involved in the conflict, and Russia and China would side with Iran.

The next message predicted the really bad news as they said that the time of turmoil would last for ten years. Their last statement seemed to make sense and be a bit more positive:

Amid all the turmoil, be happy and you will suffer least.

The session ended on a positive note with the statement:

Go in peace and be happy with the Lord.

In one of our previous sessions, we'd received the message:

God always wins.

It appears as though when the free will of humans gets them in over their heads, there is Heavenly intervention.

At the end of September 2012, several weeks after the assassination of our ambassador, we made contact with a General Guide named Charles. I first inquired if the act of violence marked the beginning of the time of turmoil. His answer was:

Yes, it will come in waves.

I also asked what would be the next event. Our guide answered:

After the elections, look for a holy war.

Trying to be optimistic, I asked if there was any chance there would not be a war and the answer was:

No.

On that down note, I asked if this was the beginning of WW3 and the answer was in the affirmative.

My next question was a bit philosophical: "Why do wars take place?" The answer was pretty much what I expected:

War is a result of not listening to God.

Looking for a light at the end of the time of turmoil tunnel, I asked if anything good would come of the war and the answer was:

Peace.

I was afraid to ask how long the peace would last. The entire session with Charles was pretty much a reiteration of what we had been hearing for the previous six months.

During a channeling session in early 2012, we received an interesting perspective on the upcoming war from one of our most famous members of the military. We were privileged to have the spirit of General Matthew Ridgeway, commander of NATO troops during the Korean War, come forward to give us his feelings about current events. General Ridgeway was a true American hero with an unblemished record. When I asked him if Israel would attack Iran on its own, the answer was:

Yes, Iran wants to play the victim.

When asked if the attack would be before our 2012 election, the answer was:

I think not.

I also asked if the conflict would turn into WW3. His answer was the same as we were hearing from other spirit sources:

It will slowly mount to WW3.

I inquired if the homeland would be attacked, to which the General replied:

From within, by Muslim cells, but nothing that cannot be handled.

My next question was if the time of turmoil would last for ten years and the reply was:

Approximately.

One thing the spirits of patriots of the past have in common is their love for the United States and the freedoms that we enjoy. None of them are satisfied with the direction our country is headed at the present time. General Ridgeway delivered the message:

We watch from here, the country dying a slow death.

He also said:

Name me one reliable leader that is out there now.

When I asked if they are observing what is happening from the other side, the answer was:

We are watching very diligently.

Barbara Lee's husband, John, was sitting at the table with us. At this point of the session, the message came through:

Westy says hi to John.

I immediately posed the question, is that General Westmoreland? The pointer spelled out:

Yes, I am.

Not only did we have the commander of the Korean War present, on this particular night, we also had one of the commanders of the Vietnam War! I asked if General Westmoreland had any messages to which the reply was:

He is in the background.

Apparently, the great generals stick together on the other side and continue to attempt to lead the nation in the right direction.

As I have stated before, we have heard this type of message concerning the upcoming conflict in the Middle East on multiple occasions. The guides want us to pass on the prediction of turmoil, so believers can prepare accordingly. Although it appears the homeland will escape most of the ravages of war, the secondary implications are many. They will include food shortages, high gas prices, and a crashing stock market. The guides have warned of Muslim uprisings and riots that will accompany the war in the Middle East, but our forces will be capable of handling the unrest. Forewarned is forearmed.

Drastic Times in the U.S.

While the threat of WW3 in the Middle East, with the emasculation of our ally Israel, seems a potent prediction of the future, we are receiving multiple warnings of an event that will have a more imminent drastic affect on the United States. In April 2012, I asked the question whether there would be a time when we lose electrical power in the United States. The answer was:

Yes.

...and when I asked the time frame, the answer was:

Winter.

In response to the previous answers, I inquired why we would lose power and the pointer spelled out:

Disruption in the atmosphere.

Next, I asked when and how long the power failure would last. The Spirit Guide replied:

Approximately December; figure approximately 3 weeks.

They never made any prediction as to what year the power failure would take place.

My belief is that the disturbance in the atmosphere, sometime in the future, will be a solar flare. If you check out the NASA Internet site, you will find that solar flares generally rise and fall in an eleven-year cycle. In 2014, the charts indicated a double peak in sunspot activity. If predictions are correct, sunspot activity should decrease for the next several years.

A little-known historical event occurred in 1859 that may shed some light on the severity or danger of a solar flare. Known as the Carrington Flare, it was the largest solar flare to hit the earth in recorded history. The rare, white light solar flare unleashed a charged plasma storm on our hemisphere that lasted for two days. It was so powerful that the telegraph lines of the time actually caught fire, shocking the operators with electrical charges. Newspapers reported the aurora was seen as far south as Cuba. Statistically, this type of event has a probability of occurrence that equals once every 100 years. A statistician would predict that such an event is overdue.

It is a well-known fact that our power grids are overloaded and vulnerable. Transmission lines would act as large antennas that would pass the charge back to delicate control panels. In addition, consider the vulnerability of our satellites to such a huge plasma surge. We would lose GPS and communication satellites as worldwide communications came to an abrupt halt. In a national power blackout, there would be no telephones, security systems, emergency services, banking transactions, and social services, to name a few. Without electricity, there will be no sewer and water service. Garbage and human waste will pile up in the streets, causing widespread sickness, and no medical care will be available.

There will be no delivery system for social payments as well as nowhere to spend money. As the days turn into weeks, there will be general panic and rioting as emergency government services cannot keep up with the growing public unrest. Citizens will not be able to replenish prescriptions as the supply of critical medical supplies diminish. Drug and grocery stores will be ransacked as unprepared citizens take food, drugs, and water anywhere they can find it. Mother Nature might accomplish what enemy countries cannot!

In our session at the end of September 2012, we asked Charles if there would be a disturbance in the atmosphere and once again he answered in the affirmative. When questioned if it would be over the Christmas Holidays, his answer was:

Approximately.

When I asked him how long it would last, the answer was:

A couple of weeks, hard to pinpoint.

Our guest then asked if we should buy a generator. Charles replied:

Good idea.

It seems that no matter how you ask the questions, there will be a tough holiday season sometime in the future.

Having done some research on the subject of fluctuations in solar storms, I asked if the disturbance would be due to solar flares. I was not expecting him to answer

2 things: solar flare and a shift.

Not understanding what the shift entailed, I asked if the shift would have a direct effect, to which he replied:

Many changes already.

I followed up by asking if there would be earthquakes and tidal waves. His answer was:

Yes, a major wave in California.

In November of 2012, I asked another guide when there will be devastating earthquakes in California and his answer was

You are asking questions that are imminent.

Next, I inquired if it would happen within two years and the answer was:

It will.

One of our female guests asked if the guide could give us anything positive. His answer attempted to interject a bit of humor:

It is all told in the good book, my dear.

I quickly asked what verse and his reply was:

Book of Revelations.

Personally, I don't find much in the Book of Revelations to cheer me up. I followed this with the question: "Will God's followers be affected by this?" The answer was:

Yes, some sacrifice must always be made.

We also attempted to get verification of forecasts of the natural disasters. The answer was not what I was expecting:

Could happen; one never knows about Mother Nature and not even God will give you even money on her. She's a Karma all her own.

This is the first time we hear that there really is a Mother Nature and she is not to be messed with! On second thought, maybe it is just the unpredictability of her character. In either case, she is not to be messed with. I guess global warming and pollution would fall under the category of messing with Mother Nature.

We have been warned of a power failure caused by a disturbance in the atmosphere. It is forecast to occur around the Christmas holidays, at some time in the future. We have been told of this event, on multiple occasions, by both the earthbound souls and General Guides. Now we are being warned of earthquakes and tsunamis. There also seems to be little doubt about a major conflict in the Middle East and ten years of turmoil in the future. The guides have been very clear that they want us to prepare for the upcoming time of turmoil and to tell others of the future predictions.

The Risk of Predictions

The risk in printing a prediction is that if it does not come true, your reputation is destroyed. Perhaps the most notable prediction that came true was given to Barbara Lee and me during a session in May 2012. The message came from a Master Guide named Ray, who was delivering the messages of St. Thomas Aquinas. We were told:

The Pope will wish to leave on his own before his time.

In February 2013, for the first time in 650 years, a Pope resigned. I'd posted this prediction on my website long before the event took place. In this instance, the Master Guides proved their ability to look into the future.

Personally, I hope *none* of these predictions come true and everyone can point their finger and laugh about the thought of a massive power failure and war in the Middle East. For my part, I will continue my preparations, including a clean pair of knickers and maybe a gun in my glove box, for a time of turmoil. In addition, and most importantly, I know that our ultimate fate is in the hands of God and all major events are preordained by an all-knowing deity and, apparently, Mother Nature.

Tracking and Predicting Mother Nature

We have been warned by the guides to watch for natural changes. Here is a list of web sites and ways to monitor the latest activities of Mother Nature and to protect yourself accordingly.

www.spiritspredict.com

Check out our website www.spiritspredict.com and join our mailing list. In our channeling sessions, we are continuously asking the guides for predictions concerning natural calamities. In November 2013, we posted online that there would be an earthquake in Puerto Rico. A 6.4 magnitude earthquake occurred on January 12, 2014. We will notify our subscribers when we are given a new prediction.

Survival Kits

Be prepared when an emergency strikes. Have access to a survival kit that can get you through a natural or man-made emergency. Here are some websites to shop for emergency supplies.

- www.amazon.com/b?node=376284011. This site lets you shop and compare a large variety of emergency and survival kits.
- http://www.ready.gov/build-a-kit. A variety of important information.

The Sun

Monitor the activity of the sun. The sun unleashes great amounts of energy toward the Earth capable of disrupting our energy grid and communications. These sites can give you advanced warning when solar events take place.

- http://spaceweather.com. This site has a subscription service that will call your phone when there is a major event taking place on the sun that will effect Earth.
- www.almanac.com/sunspotupdate. Updates for sunspots are provided by this site.
- http://solarscience.msfc.nasa.gov/predict.shtml. A NASA site for varied predictions.

Earthquakes

The prediction of earthquake activity is in its very early stages and quite primitive at best. These websites give good information.

- http://pubs.usgs.gov/gip/earthq1/predict.html
- https://sslearthquake.usgs.gov/ens/. Receive notification of earthquakes from the USGS.
- http://earthquaketrack.com/r/yellowstone-nat-park-wyoming/recent. Track earthquakes in Yellowstone National Park, the most geological active area in the United States.

Chapter 11

Voices from the Deep

Spirits that participated in historical events want to be remembered. As we were to find out, while time marches on and memories fade, the souls on the other side have their own methods of keeping the past alive. One of our sessions in 2010 would leave a lasting memory, not only for our guests, but for everyone involved.

Our experiences have shown that a large number of guests bring spirits of loved ones or deceased comrades into the room, desirous of making contact with the living. Barbara Lee can usually sense the spirit presence and help with the conversations on the Ghost Box. It is not uncommon that she can actually visualize the spirit presence. In many instances, we can usually see the presence in the form of orbs on the special cameras that are installed in the viewing room.

Previous sessions had yielded impressive results as our guests heard the voices of deceased family members. On this particular evening, thunderstorms had passed through the area earlier in the day leaving high humidity and energy in the air. Conditions created a perfect situation for spirit interaction on our Ghost Box. Spirits need to draw energy from some source and my experience has shown that the passing of electrical storms can produce amazing results. The energy of a full moon can also result in favorable interaction. Even though we had a small group on this night, I felt there would be memorable results. As it turned out, I was not disappointed.

On this night, we had a friend attending the session with his wife. Currently a fellow antique dealer, I was soon to discover that he had been in the submarine service during the heart of the Cold War with the Soviet Union. I was also about to find out that a twist of fate saved his life in the early 1960s.

Rusty and the USS *Thresher*

About thirty minutes into the spirit box session, the name "Rusty" came over the box. Our small group was at first puzzled by the name. Barbara Lee inquired if the name

"Rusty" meant anything to those present in the room. As we discussed the possibilities, my guest suddenly remembered a long-lost friend from when he had served in the submarine service.

His friend, with the nickname "Rusty" because of his red hair, had been aboard the USS *Thresher*, a nuclear attack submarine that was lost at sea on April 10, 1963, while performing a deep-water training mission. Apparently suffering a rupture in the piping system that caused the submarine to sink and implode, the ship still lies 220 miles off the coast of Cape Cod in 8,400 feet of water. The ship's complement of 16 officers and 96 seamen were all lost in the waters of the Atlantic Ocean.

As our guest recounted his memories of the *Thresher*, he had actually been assigned to be aboard the ill-fated submarine. A mix-up in paperwork had occurred, preventing him from serving on the vessel, thus saving his life. He had a friend named Rusty who had been assigned in his place and was among those lost at sea. As our guest continued to relate his memory of the incident, it turned out he actually knew five of the sailors who died aboard the sub.

Barbara Lee mentioned that she knew nothing of the 1963 disaster. Being the oldest in the group, I remembered the headlines in all the newspapers describing the loss of our first nuclear submarine. With Cold War tensions at their height, there was conjecture at the time that the Russians might have caused the accident.

The submarine *Thresher* at sea. *Photograph courtesy of the US Navy.*

As my friend finished relating his story, a silence fell over the room. We once again directed our attention to the Ghost Box. The next word over the device confirmed we were in the presence of his old friends. It was: "Thresher." I voiced the question that was now on all our minds. "Rusty, are you here for our guest?" The clear answer for all to hear was: "Yes." I asked: "Were you aboard the *Thresher?*" Once again the answer was: "Yes." We were in contact with the victims of one of our worst marine disasters and they definitely wanted everyone in the room to know it.

Two more names were heard coming across the Ghost Box, both recognized by our guest. He became choked with emotion as he indicated the additional names were also his deceased friends from the sub. I asked the question whether they were "okay" and the answer came back: "Yes." They seemed satisfied with their home on the other side. My friend was overcome with grief as the long-forgotten memories, once again, were recalled. It became clear that the ghosts of these brave sailors were not going to allow their deaths to be forgotten. I thanked the spirits for coming through and attempted to end the heart-wrenching session. I turned off the Ghost Box to provide an opportunity for everyone in the room to catch their breaths.

Gertrude

Barbara Lee broke the silence with a seemingly unrelated question. She asked if anyone recognized the name "Gertrude." The medium said she was hearing the name Gertrude over and over in her head. At the time, the name Gertrude failed to stir anyone's memory. Once again, she voiced the name, but no one in the room replied that they knew anyone by that name.

I restarted the Ghost Box in an attempt to see if there were any more responses that would help us identify Gertrude. There were no additional pertinent responses, so we all moved on with the session. The appearance of the crew members of the *Thresher* had truly been one of our most memorable events to date with the Ghost Box. As you will see in the next chapter, there was much more to come on this evening.

As I drove back to our apartment that night, my mind was racing from the amazing session we had at the store. Sleep was out of the question as I replayed the incidents of the evening through my mind. About midnight, my cell phone rang. It was a very excited Barbara Lee on the phone. The news she relayed did little to help me get to sleep.

Upon arriving at her house, she researched the USS *Thresher* incident on her computer. To her amazement the code name for the submarine on the day of the tragic accident was "Gertrude." Hours earlier, this was the name that had come to her during the session and had failed to jog anyone's memory. The spirit voices from the deep had given undeniable proof of their presence by leaving the long-forgotten code name of the incident.

Chapter 12

Mom and Dad

Since Barbara Lee and I started conducting sessions involving spirit communications, one of the things I have learned is whatever happens is entirely up to the spirits. Earlier in the evening, we had all been emotionally drained by the verbal appearance of members of the crew of the USS *Thresher*.

Just as we were starting to recover from the emotion of the earlier segment, Barbara said she heard the name "Russ" on the Ghost Box. She repeated the name several times.

After what she said sunk in, I murmured the words: "That's my father." Even though I deal with the paranormal on a daily basis, I could feel the emotion welling up inside. This would be the first time one of my deceased parents had attempted to make contact with me. I could hardly speak as I said the words: "Dad, is that you?" Over the background static of the Ghost Box, you could clearly hear the word: "Yes."

My father had died from a massive heart attack in 1970, forty-two years prior. As time went on, my wife and I had just assumed that he had passed over and his spirit was moving on to whatever takes place in that dimension. My mind was racing to grasp what was happening as I made the statement: "Dad, we all thought you had passed over." His response was: "I did." Barbara Lee quickly explained that it is possible for spirits to return to the life plane for unfinished business. My guess is that Dad has returned to watch out for his family members who were still living.

A Protective Father

In order to understand the next question, I need to tell a story of an event that could have changed all aspects of my life. In the late 1970s, my wife and I lived in northern Maryland, along with our two young daughters. In order to leave our neighborhood, there was a dangerous intersection with limited sight distance. One night, Connie was at the intersection, ready to pull out into traffic, when she heard a loud voice say: "Wait." As she slammed on the breaks of her car in response to the warning, an automobile roared by at a high rate of speed, well exceeding the speed limit. Had she pulled out, Connie would have been hit broad side, probably with fatal results. The voice, whoever it belonged to, had saved her life. Since that time, we had wondered many times whose voice she'd heard on that night. She often said she thought it was my father.

Afterlife: What Really Happens on the Other Side

Getting back to the Ghost Box session, after the initial responses, I calmed down enough to ask the question: "Dad, did you save Connie's life thirty years ago?" In spite of the background static, the answer that came back on the Ghost Box was a distinct: "Yes." The mystery was now solved as to the identity of her guardian angel on a dark night in Maryland.

A conversation with a deceased family member is always an emotional event. In fact, we now make sure there are multiple boxes of Kleenex® available. As we hold the sessions at Golden Lane, I am always monitoring the well being of our guests. As my emotions grew on this night, Barbara Lee asked if I was okay. Usually, I am the one doing the asking. I now knew how my guests felt under these circumstances.

I managed to ask one more question. I said: "Dad, are you watching out for Tracey, Kim, Amanda, and Deanna (our daughters and granddaughters)?" He replied: "Yes." I had definite confirmation that my father had saved Connie's life and was taking care of my daughters and granddaughters.

As our technology progressed, Barbara Lee and I improved our success in getting detailed messages with the Spirit Board. We began to get occasional detailed messages from my father. Several months later, we were in the middle of a session on the Spirit Board when Barbara said she was hearing the name "Emory." This was the name of my grandfather and my father's middle name. I asked if the spirit of my dad or grandfather were present in the room. In answer to my question, the pointer spelled out:

Both.

I must admit I did not expect the spirits of both of them to be present.

Next, I inquired if there was anything they would like to say. The glass pointer spelled out:

Just watching how you do this.

The spirits of my family were as interested in what was going on as we were! My next question was actually a little stupid. I inquired if he was watching now and the answer was:

Yes.

Being a firm believer that family members help look out for the living, I asked if he helped watch out for our girls. Once again the answer was:

Yes.

This was the same answer he had given months earlier. Then I asked if he was with my mother, who had passed ten years earlier. His answer brought a smile to all our faces:

I am when she is nice to me.

It seems that Heaven can be a lot like life. In that plane, apparently you can still have arguments and avoid being with the person, or in this case, spirit, until you cool down.

I now asked if I should include our conversation in my book of short stories to which he replied:

Yes, expect it.

I hope he is satisfied with this chapter. Then I inquired if I would be able to talk to him again. The answer was:

Love to Sonny.

(Sonny was a name my Mother used to call me when she was kidding, knowing it never failed to get a negative comment.) Upon hearing the name, Connie asked: "Who is Sonny?" The next answer on the board was:

My son.

Connie broke out laughing as I tried to explain the long-forgotten nickname. She unconvincingly promised not to tell the family the secret to which I murmured a comment similar to a death threat. I asked Dad if he thought Connie could keep her mouth shut. In response, the pointer rapidly spelled out:

No, smiling.

In life, Dad loved to harass my wife and his spirit could not resist the urge to do it again after forty years. It would seem that you still can have a good sense of humor in Heaven. The session ended with everyone, human and spirit, having a good laugh.

The next week we were channeling and Barbara Lee said that she heard the name "Polly." My mother's name was Pauline and her friends called her Polly. Mother was making her spirit presence felt. The pointer started out by spelling out:

Hi there.

I asked her if she has seen how my granddaughters have grown up. Her answer was:

Yes, I see them often, they are very lovely.

Connie then said that she was very proud of them to which my mother answered:

Me too.

After the usual question asking if she was okay, I asked her if she sees Dad very often. Her answer was:

Yes, when he is not cranky.

My guess is that she heard Dad's reply the week earlier and was going to fire a shot back. I asked if she was with her father, knowing that they were especially close in life. Her answer was:

Yes, wonderful man, very nice.

Even though my grandfather passed when I was only nine years old, that is exactly how I remembered him. She ended the session by saying:

Bye son and all. Love to you.

Once the spirits become accustomed to communicating on the Spirit Board, the frequency of contact increased. By the summer of 2012, it was becoming quite common to get messages from my parents. Connie and I had taken a vacation in which we drove our granddaughters across the country and through parts of Wyoming. We had more companions in the car than I realized.

Ann

The session on that August evening began by our asking for a guide of deceased souls. These are the Spirit Guides that act as gatekeepers and help bring the messages through on the talking board. The pointer spelled out the name "Ramy," a name that was unfamiliar to us. We next asked if he was a guide for deceased souls and the answer was:

Yes.

At this point of the session, I realized we could count on hearing from earthbound spirits, so I asked if there were any messages for anyone in the room. The pointer spelled out the name:

Ann.

I inquired who the message was for and the answer was:

You.

Ann was married to my first cousin and has appeared before. I then asked if she was with my dad. The pointer printed out:

Yes.

I thanked Ann for coming through again and then asked if Dad had a message. The pointer then spelled out the word:

Hello.

I inquired whether my mother was along and the answer was:

No.

My guess is that they were having a Heavenly disagreement, again. I thought I would change the subject.

Connie and my father had a very good relationship. He loved to tease her, better known as "pulling her chain." I would also point out that he was quite good at it. So I asked if he had anything he would like to say to Connie, who was close by taking notes. My question was met with a question for her:

Are you taking good care of my son?

Before I could come up with a smart answer, she replied: "You know I am."

There was no way I was getting in the middle of this conversation!

We had just driven back from our home in Utah two days before, a trip of almost 2,100 miles.

I asked if he was with us on the trip. His answer was:

Yes, it was fun.

Dad always enjoyed a good road trip. My next question was if he was with us on the road trip through Wyoming and Montana with our oldest daughter and her family. The pointer rapidly spelled out:

Yes.

Next, I asked if he enjoyed the girls and he replied one more time:

Yes.

It certainly appears that you're rarely alone, and the spirits of deceased family members are never far away.

One true sign that you are getting up in years is when your granddaughter gets a learner's permit to drive a car. While home in Park City, Connie had allowed our oldest granddaughter, Deanna, to drive her car. My next question was whether Dad had been along when she drove my wife's little convertible. The pointer now spelled out:

No, women drivers.

Then it went to the question mark:

?

After we all stopped laughing, I inquired if there was anything else he wanted to say to Connie. He confirmed what we all knew by answering:

No, she knows I love her.

When I asked if there was anything else he wanted to say, he ended the session by saying:

Not at this moment; goodbye.

As I write this story, I am touched by both the humor and continuing love displayed by my deceased family, much as it was in life.

If you, the reader, are similar to Connie and I, there are many special moments in life where you wish a deceased loved one could have been present to observe an event. Sessions with the Ghost Box and Spirit Board have shown that our departed family members actually keep pretty close contact with the living. They may act as observers or warn us in times of danger. As we found out, my father actually accompanied us on the last vacation with our daughter and grandchildren. The next time you are at a special event and say: "I wish my father or mother could be here," they probably are. Love truly crosses the veil between life and death.

Chapter 13

An Interview with Ulysses S. Grant

An underlying theme of this book of short stories is that in many instances, events in our incarnate lives are prearranged by spirits in the afterlife to help deliver their messages. This story tells of a series of events that took place over a year that resulted in two channeling sessions in which we communicated with Ulysses S. Grant, Civil War general and President of the United States.

While researching my prior book about the Battle of Gettysburg, I found that although Civil War historians don't often take to paranormal references, Larry Clowers from the *Civil War News* was complimentary of the book in his review. I researched Mr. Clowers on the Internet and found that he was not only a Gettysburg resident, but he and his wife were living history re-enactors who portrayed General Ulysses Grant and his wife, Julia. One day, I was sitting in my office at the store and somebody looking a lot like General Grant walked through the door. He introduced himself and his wife as Larry and Connie Clowers. He said no one had ever thanked him for a review before as I had and he thought they would stop by and introduce themselves. I think the reader can start to see where I am going with the "coincidence" thing.

Larry told us that he had been participating in living history in the role of Ulysses Grant for many years and he had studied the general and president in detail. His wife, Connie (note the similarity to my wife's name), portrayed Grant's wife, Julia. Although Larry was not in uniform, there was a striking resemblance. We had a nice conversation and, as they left, we talked about doing dinner sometime.

I mentioned that we had met the couple through Barbara Lee. It turns out that she knew them quite well from her activities around Gettysburg. I was beginning to think it really was a small world. It was about to get a lot smaller.

Now we started bumping into the couple on a random basis. We went into McDonalds for an iced mocha and they were standing in the lobby. Several days later, Barbara Lee came to one of our sessions and told me she ran into the couple at a banquet and sat next to them. It was almost like we were being followed.

Since I have become more sensitive to the spirit world, I find that messages are delivered while in near sleep state just as you are waking up in the mornings. Whenever I wake up with a vivid idea or thought, I usually find there is something or someone behind it. One morning, I woke up with the idea that Ulysses Grant wanted to communicate with Larry Clowers, his living alter ego. I told my wife we were going to talk with Ulysses Grant at one of our channeling sessions and she promptly replied that I was crazy. (Sometimes I wonder why people keep using the word *crazy* in my presence.)

As soon as I arrived at the store I emailed Larry and suggested that we might be able to contact the spirit of General Grant at one of our channeling sessions. About one hour later, Larry and his wife came through the door of the store with big smiles on their faces. He thought it was a great idea and I reserved a spot for them at our next channeling session.

I called Barbara Lee and told her that I was confident we could unite the spirit of Ulysses Grant with Larry Clowers. I can't remember her exact answer, but I think once again the word *crazy* was part of it. The thought of being able to get detailed messages from a past president of the United States was a bit overwhelming for my clairvoyant friend. The more I thought about it, the more confident I became that the whole series of events had been arranged by the spirits and talking to the spirit of the general was preordained.

An Interesting Session with Grant

It was finally show time; the night of the channeling session arrived. During the time leading up to the session, I had been approached by a professor of Theology who was doing scholarly research on ghost tours in the Gettysburg area. I scheduled her to also attend the session. If we pulled this off, she would make one heck of a witness, not to mention that I might get a little free publicity. As the session began, I made sure the camera and audio recording equipment were working. If the general appeared, no one would believe this without proof.

General Ulysses Grant at Cold Harbor.
Photograph courtesy of the U.S. Archives.

Barbara Lee and I sat down at the Spirit Board and placed our fingers on the glass pointer. After our usual prayer that no evil spirits come forward, I asked if a guide could bring us the spirit of Ulysses S. Grant. The pointer spelled out the word:

Hold.

We had seen this message before. Maybe the guides page the name of a spirit over a Heavenly address system. The next words spelled by the glass were:

What can I do for you?

The spirit of the Civil War Commander of the Union Army and the 18th President of the United States Ulysses S. Grant was present in our room. We were about to begin one of the most memorable interviews of our lives.

I started out by asking the president whether he was pleased with the way Larry interpreted his life at living history events. The answer brought a smile to the faces of everyone present.

Absolutely, there are a few differences, but none of major significance.

Next, I inquired as to whether the general was satisfied with the way they portrayed his wife, Julia. His answering message was:

Most assuredly.

The pair of re-enactors had done such a great job, they had attracted the attention of the spirit of the general himself. The question was asked if the general watched over Larry and Connie when they did the living history events. His reply was:

I do and I am grateful for the honest portrayal.

(This was a positive reference that they would have trouble explaining to other people without the risk of being committed to an asylum.)

I could not help jumping in to ask if my suspicions were correct with all the synchronicities that led up to this session. I blurted out:

Did you arrange for tonight?

The message supported my suspicions:

Yes, I did. Have been watching this fellow for a while now.

Larry and Connie Clowers as they portray the Grants. *Photograph courtesy of Victorian Photography Studio.*

Afterlife: What Really Happens on the Other Side

This was the first time we had real confirmation that a spirit could actually alter events in the life plane to achieve their goals. The General clearly wanted to get a message to the individuals who gave such a heartfelt portrayal to the lives of the former president and his wife. I thought back to all the events that took place to allow Barbara Lee and myself the ability to provide the channel for direct communication between individuals on both sides of the veil that separates life and death. Every time I think I am beginning to understand the spirit world, I realize how little I really know.

In life, General Grant enjoyed a good cigar. It was a cancer from his smoking that actually led to his death. Larry was prepared for the encounter and pulled a cigar out of his shirt pocket. He said: "General, I have a present for you," while he laid the cigar across the corner of the Spirit Board. The General responded:

Lord knows I haven't had one of those in a good while.

I already knew that Heaven was politically correct and there was no smoking from messages we received in prior sessions. Mayor Bloomberg would be proud.

During Grant's life, he had been accused of being a drunk by his political enemies and the rumors have persisted after his death. Larry now asked if the rumors were true, and if he should continue to try to clear his name of the accusations. The spirit answered:

I did have a bit of a problem for a time. However, a drunk I was not.

By this time, I was sure he knew there was no alcohol in the afterlife—another tidbit I picked up in prior sessions.

The night Lincoln was assassinated at Ford's Theatre, Grant was not present. An inquiry into the motives brought this reply.

*At that time, you need to understand I was
not fully in consideration with his ideas.*

History shows that by the end of the Civil War, Lincoln and Grant had differences of opinion. I followed this with an inquiry as to whether there were any regrets over his presidency.

Yes, I could have done more.

Historians view the Grant presidency as being lackluster. The abilities that made him a great general were sometimes a deterrent to his performance as president, especially during the difficult period of reconstruction of the South. The next question probed into whether he wanted to be president. The answer was abrupt:

No.

It was his wife, Julia, who wanted him to be president. Another question was whether he would rather be addressed as general, instead of president. His answer was:

I do.

This reply indicated his opinion of being president had not changed in the afterlife.

Probing Questions

Larry continued to ask probing questions that only the spirit of the general could have answered. While fighting in the Western Campaign, General Halleck, his commander, had removed Grant from command. Pressure from Lincoln forced Halleck to reinstate the best, and most successful, fighting general in the West. Halleck tried to hide the fact from Grant that he had been behind the demotion. The question was asked: "When General Halleck betrayed you, did you forgive him?"

The answer was:

Forgave but never forgot...I learned to trust no one.

As Grant received promotions, Halleck actually became a helpful ally, but Grant clearly never turned his back again.

In 1864, General Sherman's army waged a war of total destruction in his march through Georgia. The burning of Atlanta stands out as one of the more infamous events. Grant was asked his opinion of Sherman's march on the South.

I was not in agreement with annihilation.

Grant is generally assumed to have been in favor of the all-out war policy.

Grant had no love for General George H. Custer. The cavalry officer had testified before a congressional committee accusing the president's brother, Orville, of committing fraud along with Grant's Secretary of War, William Belknap. When the 7th Cavalry was sent west to fight the Indians in Montana, Grant attempted to have Custer removed from command. Grant's son was scheduled to accompany Custer on his expedition, but his orders were cancelled because of the president's lack of trust in the flamboyant cavalry officer. Otherwise, his son would have been killed at the Battle of the Little Big Horn.

Only political pressure forced Grant to reinstate Custer to rejoin the 7th. We asked what the Spirit thought of the Cavalry General. The glass pointer flew to the letters so fast, it was difficult to keep our fingers on it as it spelled out.

Custer was a damn fool.

Afterlife: What Really Happens on the Other Side

After the news of the Little Big Horn arrived in Washington, D.C., Grant said:

I regard Custer's massacre as a sacrifice of troops, brought on by Custer himself that was wholly unnecessary—wholly unnecessary.

If forgiveness is a requirement to move on, the General may still have a little forgiving to do.

Larry asked the general what were his greatest regrets. The General replied:

My greatest regret was Cold Harbor and I cannot forgive myself for my actions; I made mistakes.

During the battle of Cold Harbor, Grant's troops attacked the heavily fortified forces of Robert E. Lee with horrific results. When the battle ended, almost 7,000 Union soldiers were killed or missing and no advantage had been gained by the Federal troops. Apparently, his decisions on this day still weighed heavily on the General.

Portrait of Julia Grant. *Photograph courtesy of U.S. Archives.*

Grant's wife, Julia (portrayed by Larry's wife, Connie), came from a well-to-do economic background. She was born at White Haven Plantation, west of St. Louis, Missouri. Her father was a wealthy plantation owner and slave holder. When they were first married, living on the soldier's pay proved to be a bit of a problem. A strong woman, Julia insisted that she take over paying the bills of the Grant family so they could live within their budget. As a result, the General referred to her as "the boss." Larry inquired if he still referred to his wife by that nickname. The glass pointer rapidly went to two letters:

No.

I am not sure if the answer came from fear of reprisal or common sense.

Julia was the true love of his life and multiple questions were asked throughout our session about their relationship. On their two-and-one-half-year trip around the world, the couple visited Switzerland. While in the Alps, Julia played a trick on the general by hiding from him. When Grant couldn't find her, he assumed she had fallen off a cliff and went into a panic. Larry asked that if she had died, would he have died also. His answer was:

Chapter 13: An Interview with Ulysses S. Grant

I would not have been able to live without her.

Grant hated to dance during his life, so Larry asked if he danced with Julia on the other side. His answer was:

I never liked it there [meaning while alive] and it still stands.

Things don't seem to change a whole lot from the way they were in life on the other side.

Ulysses Grant passed in 1885 at the age of 63 from throat cancer. His body was interred at Grant's Tomb in New York City. We discussed details of his death and how he was progressing on the other side. The question was asked if he had met Jesus. His answer was:

I am not entirely there yet.

General Grant had a very slow and painful death from a cancer of the mouth. He was unable to eat, became emaciated, and probably died of malnutrition. Larry asked if it was hard to pass from this life. His answer was:

Not at all; I was resigned to it.

We have been told many times there is no pain on the other side and the general must have looked forward to an end to his suffering.

Throughout our messages with the general, it was obvious that the spirit still had a strong love for his country. One message he gave us was:

Please let all know that I love all Americans, North and South.

When we asked what he thought of what was happening in Washington, D.C., he replied:

They need to be removed. Hopefully not another war.

I could not have answered that question any better myself.

He was then asked if he saw a bright future for the United States and replied:

A lot of hard work ahead.

General Grant seems to completely understand the political problems that continue to plague our nation. "A lot of hard work ahead" may have been an understatement. Realizing that we were coming to the end of the session, Larry asked if he would ever meet the general. His reply was:

One day.

When the time comes for Larry to pass into the next dimension, he is going to have one heck of a welcoming committee.

At the end of the interview, Larry asked if there were any messages that he wanted carried into their living history events. His reply was:

There must be peace among the ranks; I have enjoyed our time together.

During his lifetime, the general had witnessed the most horrific war ever fought on the North American continent. His two terms as president coincided with the bitterness of reconstruction. Ulysses Grant lived a life of honor and expected honesty from those around him. On this particular evening in July, we had been selected to have the spirit of this great American in our presence. I marveled that the final words of such a fierce warrior called for peace among the ranks. Unfortunately, I am afraid that his warning about hard work ahead will be the most accurate prophecy.

Since the Grant interview, I've had several discussions with the Clowers concerning the impact on their lives since the interaction with the general. Whenever they are participating in a living history event, Larry has the distinct feeling that the general is with him. He feels that audience questions are answered as if the spirit puts words in his mouth.

During a recent trip to Italy, they actually retraced the visit made by the Grants almost 150 years earlier. Larry stated that on many occasions, it was like he had visited the places before and actually had the ability to find his way without any familiarity of the area. Their supernatural bond seemed to be strengthening.

About six months passed and I was running errands in the town of Gettysburg. It was a little after 11 a.m., but I decided to stop by the recently remodeled McDonalds and get a quick lunch. As I looked at a corner table, I realized that Larry and Connie Clowers were sitting in a corner booth reading a newspaper. As I walked over to say hello, the thought went through my mind that General Grant wanted to talk to them again. The mental message was loud and clear. I had no doubt that the former president of the United States was not finished with the couple.

As we began to talk, they mentioned that they, too, had never been in the new McDonalds before and had made a spur-of-the-moment decision to stop by for a cup of coffee. The more we talked, the clearer it became in my mind that our meeting was the result of supernatural manipulation. I made arrangements for them to attend a channeling session with Barbara Lee the next Saturday night.

A Spirit Possession

We began the session asking for a master guide. Almost immediately, one our regular guides, Martin, came through and we spent around a half-hour receiving political predictions. Larry was sitting between Barbara Lee and myself. He started to say that he was getting a bad headache and, as we watched, seemed to go into a trance-like state.

His hands began to shake and he began to breathe heavily. I grabbed his shoulder in fear that he was having a major physical problem. Barbara Lee seemed to realize what was happening and made the sign of the cross on his forehead. She asked if he was really Larry or another spirit had taken over his body. I suddenly realized that we were observing full-blown spirit possession! Larry Clowers had lost total control of his physical actions and was going into a deep trance!

With trembling hands, he reached for the glass used to spell out messages on the spirit board while Barbara Lee and I watched in amazement. The glass began to move with only Larry's hand upon it! In his attempt to spell out a message, the glass fell from his hand. He immediately grabbed it again and began to deliver some type of message. Whatever spirit possessed his body, it definitely had something it wanted to say and our guest was about to deliver it. I asked the guide what was happening to Larry and the answer was:

You asked for a prominent person in history.

Orville Grant Appears

My next question was whether Ulysses Grant was present, but there was no answer. While Larry was attempting to spell out the message, Barbara Lee began to hear messages in her head. She asked if he is General Grant's brother, but there was no answer on the board. Once again, she said that she was hearing a mental message that Larry is General Grant's brother, Orville, reincarnated. Our guest went into a deeper trance and once again grabbed for the glass. He spelled out the message:

He is here with us.

Barb quickly asked if Larry is Orville reincarnated and the answer on the board was:

Yes.

Unable to totally grasp what was happening, I asked if Orville is Larry Clowers in this life and once again the answer was:

Yes.

The soul of Orville Grant, brother of Ulysses Grant, had reincarnated in the body of Larry Clowers and was attempting to deliver a message!

Let me digress for a moment and give the reader a little more historical background. As president of the United States, Ulysses Grant's administration had been plagued with multiple scandals. In 1876, General George Custer had testified before Congress that the current Secretary of War, William Belknap, had participated in a kickback scandal where traders at Army Posts on the Indian reservations were supplying troops with defective weapons and hostile Indians with superior weapons for profit. Custer implicated the brother of the president, Orville, in the scandal. The President reacted by getting rid of everyone involved, including his own brother. Custer was removed from command for blowing the whistle on the President's brother, but was reinstated just in time to participate in the Battle of the Little Big Horn. Unfortunately, he found out for himself just how accurate his testimony was about the Indians having superior weapons.

Getting back to our channeling session, Larry was in a deep trance and had the glass in his hand. I asked what the spirit had to tell us and the glass spelled out the message:

Grant will return soon.

Are you saying that Grant will be reincarnated and return to an incarnate life soon, I asked? The answer to that question was:

Yes.

We had previously been told that a man of God would be coming soon. I asked if Grant would be that man. The spirit answered:

Maybe, you will see.

Brother Apologizes to Brother

Barbara Lee sensed the presence of the spirit of Ulysses Grant present in the room and asked if there was anything Orville would like to say to General Grant. Larry now had the glass in his hand and spelled out the message:

Will you forgive me for what I did to you? I betrayed my brother.

While Larry was spelling out the message, his face reflected the picture of grief and tears were streaming down his face. He remained in a deep trance and had no idea of his actions.

At the time of the session, I was not familiar with the historical facts concerning what happened between the two Grant brothers. I asked why he betrayed his brother and the answer was:

For money.

"When did you betray your brother?" The spirit of Orville answered:

Scandal with Custer.

Next, I asked what he did and the reply was:

Sell influence, for money, forgive me; I love you.

I asked if it was during the presidency and the answer was:

Yes.

Larry's wife, Connie, interjected the question, "Was it a Ponzi scheme?" The reply was:

No, Belnap.

All the answers were historically accurate.

Ulysses Accepts Orville's Apology

Larry now let go of the glass and appeared to be starting to come out of the trance. Barbara Lee and I placed our fingers on the glass and I asked if the spirit of General Grant was present.

I am here. I have known and have been waiting for my brother to tell me. I have been with Lawrence knowing he is my lost brother. I have been in pain for many years, hurting.

As if that wasn't enough of a revelation, Barbara now hears in her head that "Larry" is too informal and that the General prefers to refer to his brother as "Lawrence." I now asked if the General could now forgive his brother. His reply was:

I have long ago. I needed to hear his confession. My brother had thoughts of suicide.

Apparently, the General had basically disowned his brother after the scandal and Orville had suffered deep depression. Next, I asked the General if he had arranged for us to meet so we could have this session tonight. His answer was what I expected:

I did. This is the only way I could tell him.

I knew my running into the Clowers at McDonald's was no accident! Making sure I got the name correct, my next question inquired if the General was with Lawrence all the time. The General replied:

When able.

Barbara now asked if Orville/Lawrence was now at peace. He answered:

Yes, I go now. I am going to rest.

This was the first time I heard of a spirit having to rest!

Larry/Lawrence now came completely out of his trance. He had no memory of what had taken place and his headache had gone away completely. I asked the General if there were any messages for Lawrence. He answered:

How do you feel? Welcome home.

An Amazing Spirit

At this stage of the session, I had no idea if the General was talking to Orville, Lawrence, or Larry. I told General Grant that he was an amazing spirit to have arranged all this. His modest reply was:

So I have been told. I will be coming back and wanted to be sure that Lawrence understands who he was and what he had done. He has my blessing to portray me because I know it comes from his heart.

I think the pieces of the puzzle were now coming together. During his lifetime, General Grant banished his brother, Orville, for participating in a scandal that embarrassed him while president. Then, during the 1950s, the spirit of Orville Grant reincarnated in the body of Larry Clowers. The spirit of Orville led the Clowers to reenact the General and Julia Grant. While on the other side, the spirit of General Grant watched, and, as the Clowers became more and more dedicated to his portrayal, he brought about events that allowed him to forgive and reunite with his estranged brother. The General, whose spirit was now under time restraints because he was about to reincarnate, used Barbara Lee and me as channels to communicate with the spirit of Orville, who now happens to reside in the body of Larry/Lawrence Clowers. At our channeling session, Orville's spirit took over the body of Larry and sought forgiveness from the spirit of his brother, General Grant. After 140 years, the spirits of the brothers made peace with each other and are now able to move ahead with their new life paths.

Believe me folks; I am not capable of making up this kind of stuff!

The spirits on the other side of the life veil have an amazing ability to affect or alter events for those of us currently on the incarnate side. Larry and Connie Clowers continue to portray the Grants with a passion that can only be the result of a supernatural guidance. As we have all learned, the guidance from above is real and neverending. A major regret is that I will not be able to live long enough to see the results of the reincarnation of Ulysses S. Grant.

Chapter 14

Protect Us From Evil

We all know that evil exists in many forms. It exists in the afterlife, as well as the three dimensions we occupy here on Earth. If you have any doubts, watch the evening news to see proof of how it envelopes our daily lives. Since all incarnate beings have free will, evil is only held in check by one's belief structure or laws enacted to direct personal behavior. For many of us, fear of retribution when we get to the other side plays a large role in current personal behavior. As you will learn in this chapter, religious beliefs and faith are the only things that will protect us from the spirit energy of evil.

If you look at the definition of evil, it usually deals with some type of immorality. A religious interpretation would be that it is any action contrary to the character or teachings of God. I am not sure how an atheist would define evil, but it probably ties into some type of bad behavior. If you don't believe in Christ, you can't have an Antichrist.

Volumes have been written on the philosophical discussion of good and evil and I am not about to get bogged down in that type of dissertation. Instead, I am going to focus on evil as discussed by the Heavenly guides that have appeared at our various channeling sessions. After all, who is in a better position to describe evil than those on the other side of the veil of life that possess the Heavenly energy to communicate with Barbara Lee and me? They definitely have a far different perspective than those of us currently in an incarnate situation.

Bad Things A-brew

My first contact with the Spirit Guides concerning the presence of evil occurred in February 2011 during a channeling session with our clairvoyant friends in Utah. Here are the exact words of the guides from that session:

We want to start explaining that there is, is, is, is, bad things out there. Yes, and how to keep them out of what you are doing. Rule number 1: never invite bad or evil in. It tends to stay if not quickly asked to exit. Let bad know you do not want them about you.

They never gave me a rule number 2, so I assume that rule number 1 is quite important. As I was to learn, it seems to be the only rule concerning the avoidance of evil.

One evening, at a session in New Oxford, we asked a Master Guide how to recognize evil forces. His reply was:

*Talk of God and check reactions.
Remember Satan cannot stand up against God.*

This strategy seems to work pretty well with humans, but the mention of Satan caught my attention. During another session, I asked if Satan is an actual form that can be seen. His reply was:

Satan is an energy. Lucifer is seen and is the persona of the Devil.

I can't help but think we should change the name of Washington, D.C. to Lucifer, D.C. There is enough of the persona of the Devil in that town to warrant a new name.

The bottom line here is that negative or evil energy really does exist. This energy can exhibit itself in a human or spirit form. In many instances, evil energy can be expelled by means of an exorcism. This is the practice of removing evil spirits from a person or property believed to be possessed. If you are going to get bogged down by scientific definition, demonic possession is not a valid psychiatric or medical diagnosis recognized by the medical profession. If you have a property that has an evil presence, my guess is that you really don't care what the scientific community thinks. One evening in May 2013, we had guests come to our channeling session whose home was possessed with an evil presence. Prior to that time, we had no prior knowledge of the purpose of our guests' visit or what was about to take place in our channeling of the afterlife.

The Number 3
On this particular evening, our Master Guide introduced himself as "Roy." The paranormal session began with the Heavenly spirit discussing predictions and the degeneration of faith in our country. This Master Guide had appeared to us on other occasions and provided very accurate predictions and information.

When we turned to the personal message portion of the evening, we asked our guest if he had any questions. He replied by asking: "What is the reason that everywhere I go I see the number 3?" Our guide quickly spelled out the word "code" on the Spirit Board. Neither Barbara Lee nor I had any idea what was happening or the meaning of the number 3.

In order to ask semi-intelligent questions and direct the session, I asked our guest to explain what was happening. His reply was that wherever he went, he would see the number 3 or multiple 3s. He would find 3 objects around the house. Threes would appear on the face of his cell phone. The number would keep appearing in his mind and he would dream about the number. I asked the guide why the numbers were appearing for our guest. Roy spelled out:

33 is Christ.

I did not know that Christ had his own code! Barbara spoke out that the numbers must be a sign the spirit of Christ is present and was protecting him. My next question inquired if that was good for our guest and the answer was:

Yes.

I asked our male guest to explain what was happening in his life that would require such special protections. His reply got my undivided attention. Apparently, the house in which he and his wife lived had an evil presence. A large mirror leaning against the wall had been pushed over and broken. An ashtray had been thrown across the room. One morning, his wife woke to find three scratches on her leg, too wide apart to have been left by their cats. His wife even mentioned seeing a dark cloud over their bed. It seemed like shades of Amityville! This was the first time we had been exposed to anything like this in our sessions.

In the House
Turning back to the Spirit Board, I asked the guide who was in their house. His reply was:

Elderly.

My follow-up inquiry was to find out whether the presence was evil, to which Master Guide Roy answered:

Not good.

So far we'd found out there was an elderly presence that was definitely not good. I was beginning to get an idea why our guests had come to the session on this evening. There was an awful lot happening in their lives that could not be explained and they were looking to Barbara Lee and me for answers.

My next inquiry concerned the scratch marks left on the leg of our female guest. The answer was:

Negative entity.

Next, I asked if it was a very bad spirit and the answer was:

Yes.

This bad spirit had enough negative energy to actually leave scratch marks that broke the skin! I had heard stories of persons waking up with such scratches after nightmares, but this time we were in the presence of someone that had actually suffered such a phenomenon.

There is usually a reason for the appearance of an evil spirit. I asked Roy, our guide, if it was in the house before the guests moved in. His answer was:

It was attached to a guest.

When I asked how long the presence had been in the house, the answer was:

12 years.

Next, I inquired if it came from the prior owner and the pointer spelled out:

Dabbled in darkness.

Now I began to really appreciate the advice about never inviting evil that was given to me in that first channeling session. It was becoming obvious that the previous owners had conducted some sort of satanic rituals and whatever evil presence came in with one of the participants had decided to remain with the property.

I thought I would attempt to find out more information about the evil presence, so I asked if the presence was female. Roy's answer was:

Yes.

Next, I asked what the presence wanted in the house. Our guide's message was:

To aggravate and harm.

At this point I had established that the presence was female and wanted to aggravate and harm. (I think I will let that thought pass without any further comment.)

As we continued to discuss the situation with our guests, the wife commented that, in spite of being scratched, she really did not feel any fear concerning the presence. I next inquired if the entity was a threat to the wife and the reply was:

Not a threat.

Whatever was haunting the house seemed to only be upset with the male member of the family? When I asked if the evil spirit had a name, the reply was:

I will not call it.

The guide would not even repeat the bad spirit's name for fear it would invite the presence to come forward!

Barbara Lee had participated in exorcisms in the past, so I asked the guide if she could help our guests rid their house of the evil spirit. His answer was:

If they will heed.

When I asked what we could do to help our guests, Roy replied:

They will be advised of what to do.

It was becoming obvious that the guides had brought our guests to the channeling session to get Barbara's help in ridding their place of the bad spirit. I asked one final question: "Is it preordained that the guests were brought here tonight?" Roy's answer was one word:

Yes.

On this particular evening, the Spirit Guides were using Barbara Lee and me to provide the information that would protect our guests from evil in their home.

Negative Influences

On that evening in May, we learned a lot about just how powerful the forces of evil can be and the extent to which the guides will go to prevent their appearance. After the segment on evil, we began an attempt to bring forth the spirits of other family members for our guests. Barbara Lee commented that the room seemed to be free of energy and we were not getting any responses. We had seen this happen before when there were non-believers or persons who had experimented with the dark side in attendance.

The pointer began to move and delivered a final message for the evening:

This is Roy. Having a time bringing through due to negative. Cleanse first.

The negative attachment even prevented other spirits from coming through and Roy was taking no chances on evil coming into our building! There would be no spirit communication with our guests until they followed the instructions and cleansed themselves of the evil presence. Spirit guides also act as protectors and Roy was definitely doing his job.

Barbara Lee then proceeded to give our guests the information to cleanse their home and personal energy. The purging of evil must be addressed with caution. In many instances, the exorcism can only be accomplished with the assistance of a priest or pastor who has been specifically trained to perform the task.

Since learning of the code for Christ, variations of the number 33 have been appearing for Connie and me. I placed a bid on a valuable piece of jewelry in an online auction and was surprised to find that I was the successful bidder with a winning bid of $333.00. One day, Connie checked to see the store's daily sales and the number was $3,333.33. I prefer to think these occurrences are an indicator that we are pursuing a Karma course that is meeting with approval from the other side.

It is imperative that the reader remember the quote of the guides from earlier in this chapter:

"Satan cannot stand up to God."

Without God, there is no check on evil. Keep in mind that there is no such thing as an atheist conducting an exorcism.

How to Cleanse or Exorcise a Property of Evil

Holy Water is water that has been blessed by a member of the clergy or a religious figure. It can be purchased at a religious supply store or online. Purchase enough holy water to treat the property.

- Place Holy Water around all openings to the property such as windows and doors. Start with the area of the property that has exhibited the most negative activity. Sprinkle traces of the Holy Water throughout the area.
- Purchase a white Christ candle. Purchase a white candle that represents Christ at a religious supply store. If the candle has been blessed, so much the better.
- Burn the white candle of Christ when you are present in the property for seven days.
- As you burn the candle of Christ, repeat "The Lord's Prayer" seven times in each room on each of the seven days as you sprinkle the holy water.
- Ask for protection from evil in your prayers and that the evil presence

leave the premises.

- We were told by the guides that salt welcomes good and insults the bad. Spraying with salt water will keep only the good in place. (If holy water is not available, try using salt water.) Spreading salt around the perimeter of the building will help discourage evil from entering the building.
- Always let the bad or evil know that you do not want their presence around.
- If the presence of evil persists in spite of your efforts using the procedures outlined, contact a priest or pastor experienced in performing an exorcism.
- Your only protection from evil is your strong belief in God. If you have any doubts regarding your belief structure, there will be no way to protect yourself from the energy of the dark side.

Chapter 15
The Two Stooges

The Ghost Box has generated some of our more memorable sessions at Golden Lane. In this chapter, I tell the story of multiple messages from Shemp Howard of the Three Stooges. His spirit has communicated with us both verbally and with direct messages on the Spirit Board. In addition to my audio recordings, there were ten witnesses to this hard-to-believe story.

It was a clear night in early November 2011, most notable because of the full moon. As we began the session, we had a group of eight guests in the room along with Connie, Barbara Lee, and me. When I turned on the special cameras, we could see that our room was quite active with orb activity. This usually indicates that spirits were accompanying some of our eight guests.

As we started the Ghost Box portion of the session, everyone in the room heard the distinct name of Jeffery Silverman, my spirit friend. As we moved on, one of our guests heard the names of four different family members who had passed, including her grandfather and grandmother. When Barbara and I asked questions, we were able to get multiple distinct responses from them. The answers were so strong that I accused her of bringing along a deceased family reunion. It seemed like this would indeed be a very interesting session.

Shemp Howard

As things quieted down, we all heard an unfamiliar name coming over the Ghost Box. Barbara Lee asked if anyone heard a name: Shep or Shem or maybe even Shemp. We all listened closely as once again the spirit gave his name. It sounded like "Shemp." Barbara Lee exclaimed the only Shemp she could think of was Shemp Howard of the Three Stooges. She asked the question: "Are you Shemp Howard?" The reply could be clearly heard: "Yep."

After we recovered from that surprise, she asked, "Are all you guys here?" A single word was heard: "Nope."

It was time for direct action, so I asked if he was one of the Three Stooges. His response was a clear "yes." For some reason, we had the spirit energy of Shemp Howard of the famous comedy group, the Three Stooges, with us in the room.

The next question asked was: "Is anyone else who was a member of the Stooges with you?" The answer was: "Yes." "Is Larry with you?" The answer was: "No." Barbara Lee asked the direct question: "Who is with you tonight?" The answer was: "Mo." (Moe Howard was Shemp's brother.) I had finally recovered to the extent that I asked: "Moe, can you say 'hello' for us?" Everyone heard a clear: "Hello." Not only was Shemp Howard here, he was accompanied by his brother, Moe. Next we asked if Larry was present. This time the answer was: "No." One of our guests interjected the question: "Do you still do slapstick on the other side?" The reply was: "Absolutely." It was good to know they still have a sense of humor in Heaven. I wish I had remembered to ask if they still sold tickets.

At times like this, we attempt to ask direct questions that would be only known by the deceased individuals to prove that we are really communicating with their spirits. Barbara Lee asked the question of Shemp: "Where were you born?" The answer came back: "Brooklyn." Shemp Howard was indeed born in Brooklyn, New York. The next question was: "When did you pass?" "November" came over the Ghost Box. (Shemp Howard died on November 22nd from a heart attack.) We followed-up this answer by asking if November 13th meant anything to him. The answer was "no." He wasn't about to be tripped up with a trick question. Apparently, the spirits remain very aware of information concerning their recent incarnate lives. Shemp passed the direct question test with flying colors.

At this point of the session, we had been communicating with the two stooges for over thirty minutes. A long-term event of this nature is very unusual because the spirits don't usually have the strength for multiple replies. By the end of this conversation, Shemp had recorded twenty-three individual replies over a period of thirty-three minutes, the longest spirit interview we've ever encountered. If there is caffeine in Heaven, these guys were definitely on it.

Our guests started to participate in the session. One asked if he could do a skit for us. The answer was "What?" Then someone made the statement that she thought Larry was the funniest of the group to which I joked: "Go ahead, piss him off and he won't answer any more." Over the Ghost Box you could hear a voice say: "Oh, that's nice." Apparently, they've cleaned up their act since moving on.

In the Book

Next, I tried to pursue why they had come to our paranormal session. Since I was in the process of writing this book of short stories, I asked if he was here so I would write about him in my next book. The answer was: "Yep." I then asked him if he would help me sell the book. His answer was: "That's your job." Delegation of authority seems to be no problem from the other side. There was then a period of silence where we could not hear any answers. I asked the question: "Are you still here?" The answer was: "Fortunately." Barbara Lee then said: "Say 'hello' to Curley," to which there was the reply: "I did." My guess is that they must all still stay in close contact with each other on the other side. That reply marked the end of one of the most remarkable sessions we had to date on our Ghost Box.

This was the first time we had a famous personality make an appearance at one of our paranormal events. I was glad there was a large group of witnesses to verify what had taken place. It is certainly not every day that we have an extended conversation with two of the Three Stooges! At the time, I could think of no good reason for the spirit to talk to our group.

During subsequent sessions, Barbara Lee and I tried to make additional contact with either Shemp or Moe Howard. Occasionally, we would hear faint replies, but we could never duplicate the previous extended session on the Ghost Box.

As time passed, and we became acquainted with the Spirit Board, it proved to be a powerful tool for detailed communication with the other side. One evening in March 2012, Barbara Lee and I were conducting a channeling session and she asked if Shemp could come forward. Without hesitation, the glass pointer moved to the "message for" area of the board. She had made contact with Shemp Howard. Barbara Lee then asked him why he had made contact in the past session on the Ghost Box. The pointer spelled out the word:

Remembrance.

The spirit of the famous comedian was just trying to make sure that their type of humor was being remembered by the present generation.

I jumped into the conversation by saying that I had already started to write the story of his appearance at our session and that he and Moe would have a prominent place in it. The glass pointer now spelled out the words:

Biggest smile.

The spirit seemed quite happy with his appearance in this story. With that comment, the pointer moved to the "Good bye" portion of the board and the spirit energy of our celebrity friend left the room. Once again, the Spirit Board supplied answers that would have been difficult to obtain on the Ghost Box.

Several months later, we were having dinner with our friends who own the haunted bed and breakfast Barker House in New Oxford. I brought along the Ghost Box so we could attempt to contact the prior owner of the house, whose spirit makes numerous appearances for their guests. When we turned on the instrument, I heard a quite unexpected name: "Shemp."

I quickly asked if Shemp Howard was present and the answer was: "Yes." He had followed us to our friends' bed and breakfast. Connie quickly chimed in: "I bet he is here to find out why you haven't published the book yet." "Yes," once again came over the Ghost Box. He came back to light a fire under my butt to get this book published! I guess the last time we talked over the Ghost Box, Shemp must have thought the book was ready for the publisher.

I tried to explain that the spirits were continuing to give me information and it took a lot of work to finish the book and mentioned that I would get busy and finish it. His reply was simply: "OK." This is the first time I felt bad for disappointing a spirit. Shemp must have been satisfied that his message was delivered and there were no more responses on that evening.

One thing we have found out in working with the spirits is that they do not want to be forgotten. Once they realize that we can provide a channel for them to deliver messages from the other side, they will return to avail themselves of our services. If the two Stooges repeatedly appeared at our session to have their story included in my book of short stories, they succeeded. My hope is they will continue to communicate with us, even though this chapter is finished. As Barbara Lee and I have discussed on many occasions, one thing is becoming apparent: thanks to the cooperation of the spirits, the amazing is becoming common place.

Chapter 16

Joel Took the Box

We have experimented with different scan rates or how fast the radio scans the entire AM dial when using the Ghost Box. Our experience has shown that the faster it moves through the dial, the more efficient the box is in allowing the ghosts to give a clear response. Our earlier boxes scanned at a slower rate than the equipment we are currently using. As you will see in this story, the spirits succeeded in letting us know they prefer a Ghost Box that scans at a high rate of speed.

In late September 2011, I was preparing the equipment for a session at Golden Lane and discovered that my favorite rapid scanning Ghost Box was missing from the shelf in my viewing room. At our store, when something is missing, there is always the possibility that one of our spirits has hidden the item. For instance, one time I was using a screw driver and laid it on the table where I was working in the basement. When I came back to use it, the screw driver was not where I left it and I could not locate it. The next day, I found the tool had been returned to the same place on the table. I hoped the Ghost Box would be replaced like the screw driver.

Unfortunately, the Ghost Box failed to reappear. This time, my guess was that some unscrupulous individual had figured out how to get a Ghost Box without paying for it. If the person who took it believed it was just a radio, he would be in for a rude awakening. As I set up my equipment for the next session, I was forced to bring my old Ghost Box out of retirement. It had a slower scan rate, but there was no way to get a new radio before Saturday night. Surely, the spirits would not notice the difference!

As the session began, we observed a huge number of orbs on the live cameras and the EMF meters were reflecting the activity. Everyone in the room was anticipating the Ghost Box portion of the session. Barbara Lee began the session by asking if anyone would like to come forward and speak to someone in the room. A male voice responded with "stop" in a loud voice that was heard by everyone. Not exactly what we were expecting! Barbara asked who it was who had said "stop," but there was no definitive answer.

When the room is active with orbs passing through, it is quite common to hear a lot of different names. One of the names we heard was "Joel," but none of the guests were familiar with a deceased person by that name.

All of our sessions are recorded in quad sound on a special recorder, so we have clear documentation of what takes place. I can attach earphones to the recorder and listen in live time. The amplification through the headset lets me hear the responses better and ask questions. As I listened on the earphones I clearly heard a female voice say "stop." Whatever we were doing, the spirits, male and female, obviously wanted us to stop it. The more we asked questions, the more we heard random voices say "stop." This had never happened before. Barbara and I discussed what could possibly be causing all the negative answers. It did not occur to us that we had spoiled the ghosts with the rapid scan machine and we were now using the old equipment.

I suggested that maybe the volume was too loud on the box. I turned down the volume and Barbara asked the question: "Is that better?" A clear male voice spoke the word: "No." Apparently the volume was not an issue. This was turning into a very bizarre session.

Sometimes, the direct approach works best, so I asked the question, "What would you like us to stop?" A different male voice answered: "Other box." It suddenly dawned on me that they were talking about the Ghost Box itself; they wanted us to use the other box, the one that had been stolen! Barbara Lee responded to my epiphany by saying: "Well, you will just have to make do." A male voice made the response in a disgusted tone: "Great." It seems spirits don't handle disappointment well.

My next question was: "Did someone take the box?" The clear response was: "Yes." Now we were really getting close to solving the mystery theft. I asked: "Who took the box?" The next answer was "Joel." That was the name we'd heard earlier in the session. Whoever Joel is, living or dead, he apparently stole my Ghost Box. I thought I would verify the name of the culprit, so I asked the question: "Did you say Joel stole the box?" The answer was: "Yep." Case closed! Joel never realized he was being watched from the other side as he perpetrated the crime.

One of the guests then asked what I believe was the best question of the evening. "Will you go to Joel's house and spook him and maybe get the box back?" The clear answer was: "Sure." Whoever Joel is, I think his Karma is about to take a turn for the worse. If someone comes running through the door of the store yelling, "Please take back the Ghost Box," we will know it is Joel.

Chapter 17
Still Fighting

I know from my interaction with the spirit world to expect the unexpected. Every once in a while an event will happen that is totally beyond anything we have ever experienced. Such an event happened on July 4th, 2012. This entire occurrence was so far outside our scope of understanding that the reader will find it very hard to accept my story as real. I have eight living individuals who witnessed the events of that summer evening. This is yet another instance where truth is much stranger than fiction.

To fully appreciate the events of that evening, a little historical background is required. The battle of Gettysburg began on July 1st, 1863 when a corp of soldiers under the command of General A. P. Hill advanced toward the small Pennsylvania town. A Confederate brigade, consisting of mostly troops from the state of Alabama under General James Archer, drew first blood by attacking the Union army in the vicinity of a small creek named Willoughby Run.

The initial Rebel attack was beaten back when Union reinforcements of the 1st Corp under General Reynolds arrived in time to drive back the Confederates, actually taking General Archer and 200 of his men prisoner. During this part of the battle, General Henry Heth, the Division Commander, was wounded along with the capture of General Archer, causing great confusion in the Rebel command structure. Immediate command was assumed by colonels and majors causing a delay in the fighting that allowed Union reinforcements to arrive on the field.

Overwhelming Rebel reinforcements finally overran the Union positions near Willoughby Run, driving the Army of the Potomac back to a defensive position on Cemetery Hill. After three days of fighting and 52,000 casualties on both sides, on July 4th, General Lee ordered his men to retreat back to the safety of Virginia. One of the major retreat routes, known as the Hagerstown Pike at the time of the battle, is now State Road 116. It runs through the town of Fairfield, Pennsylvania. From there, it proceeds through one of the passes of the Blue Ridge Mountains and then south toward Virginia.

This was the main retreat route for the Confederates healthy enough to fight if needed. The wounded would take the Cashtown Road in a huge caravan of wagons towards the town of Chambersburg, Pennsylvania, and then south to friendly territory below the Mason Dixon line. General J.E.B. Stuart and his cavalry defended the rear of the retreating column of the healthy soldiers from the harassing Union cavalry. A battle actually took place near the town of Fairfield in which the Union cavalry, under the command of Major Samuel Starr, was defeated, allowing the Confederate cavalry to control the Fairfield Gap.

Barbara Lee and her husband own a property that lies directly on the Lee retreat route. On the 4th of July the previous year, I had taken pictures in the vicinity of their property and recorded some interesting results. This year, Barbara and I were anxious to try the Spirit Board in an attempt to communicate with the ghosts of the Confederate soldiers. In preparation for the evening, we even flew a Southern flag, the stars and bars of the Confederacy, to help persuade any reluctant Rebel spirits that they would be welcome. What was about to happen met our expectations, and then some.

The weather was hot and humid as the sun set, and local fireworks started to appear against the night sky. We decided to try the Spirit Board on the outside picnic table, probably because it was in close proximity to the pitcher of marguerites. Having never attempted to channel in the outdoors before, I had concerns as to how effective our efforts would be on this night. Connie positioned herself to record the proceedings on her note pad.

A ghost soldier is photographed in a bayonet charge near Willoughby Run.

After saying our usual prayers to prevent any bad energy from coming through, I asked if there were any spirits present. Almost immediately, the glass pointer began to move, spelling out the words:

Colonel... Willoughby.

As I mentioned above, Willoughby Run was the scene of some of the most violent fighting on the morning of the first day. The cover picture of my first book has the image of a ghost soldier in a bayonet charge in the vicinity of the Willoughby Run fighting.

I asked: "Why are you here?" to which the spirit replied:

Troop movement.

In light of the date and location, my question may have seemed a bit stupid, but I asked if he fought in the Civil War. He answered:

War for southern independence.

Residents of the South viewed the War Between the States as a fight to become a separate country, much as their forefathers had done in their fight to overthrow the British. This was exactly how an officer of the Confederacy would refer to what Northerners call the Civil War. We had definitely made contact with a soldier of the South.

Having written a book that included a historical narrative of the battle, I have a pretty good familiarity with the beginning aspects of the fighting. My next question was quite specific, making sure we had contacted the real thing. I asked who he fought with. His reply was:

General Archer.

Wanting more details, I asked what regiment he fought with, to which he replied:

6th Alabama.

Absolutely correct; the 6th Alabama was part of General Archer's Brigade that was captured in the vicinity of Willoughby Run. We had made contact with a Confederate Colonel who had fought in the Battle of Gettysburg!

About this time, Connie started to complain that I was asking the questions too fast and she could not keep up with the notes. My adrenalin was truly pumping as I realized that I was questioning a spirit that had actually taken part in the most violent battle to ever take place on American soil! I tried to slow down, so she did not throw the pen at me. Our guide solved the problem by waiting until she recorded my question before giving his responses. Next, I asked a seemingly redundant question: "Did you fight at Gettysburg?" I should have realized there was something strange about his answer. It was:

Yes, I am here now.

Note that he answered in the present tense.

Being slow to catch on to what was really happening, I asked another redundant question: "Did you fight for the South on the first day?" His answer was once again:

Yes.

Next, I inquired into the details of his involvement in the fighting. "Did you fight near Willoughby Run?" to which he answered:

Yes, I helped replace Archer; I was wounded.

Looking for more detail, I asked if he knew the name of the field hospital where he was treated. His answer was:

I don't know.

During the battle, aid would have been given in any existing building, sometimes even in open fields, usually near water for cleansing the wounds. The battle moved so rapidly that no name would have been assigned to the field hospital. They were only named after the war.

His next statement would change the entire meaning of the interview. It was:

I am still in the fight, we are moving south.

He was answering in the present tense again! For the first time since we began our session, I became aware that it seemed like the colonel thought he was still fighting the battle. In all our experiences with the afterlife, we had never communicated with a presence that did not realize it had passed from the life plane. I inquired if he was going home to Alabama to which he answered:

No.

Having never been in a situation like this before, I tried to sort out what was happening by asking if he was passing over into Heaven. His answer was:

Cannot do.

Since it was the 4th of July, I asked if he was aware of the anniversary of the battle. None of us expected the answer:

No, we are still in the fight.

We were getting messages from a Confederate colonel who was in the exact spot he occupied 149 years ago, defending the rear of General Lee's retreating army, and he was still fighting the war!

Our group was sitting at a picnic table with enough outdoor lights to see what was taking place on the Spirit Board. The women were dressed in shorts and baseball caps, intently watching the events that were unfolding. My next question was: "Do you know what the lights are?

He answered:

Cannot explain; I am confused.

Next, I inquired: "Are you with us now?" to which he replied:

Yes, what is this?

[Referring to the Spirit Board]

That and the manner of dress. Am I dreaming?
I am not dead; I am here with my men.

Not only did the spirit of the colonel not know he had passed, he had all his men with him! He also found the dress of the women a little disconcerting. I don't think they wore shorts and baseball caps during the 1860s.

My next inquiry was: "Who do you think we are?" His answer was:

Do not know. Tell me more. We are right here
with you, can you not see us. Imboden has gone ahead.

General John Imboden commanded a troop of cavalry totaling approximately 2,000 men. He arrived on the field late morning of July 3rd, as Lee was preparing for the assault that became known as Pickett's Charge. He did not actually participate in the Battle of Gettysburg. Since his troops were fresh, Lee assigned Imboden to guard and protect the retreat of the wagon train containing almost 13,000 wounded. This turned out to be a monumental task, since the wounded occupied 1,200 wagons and stretched over 14 miles. To make matters worse, a driving rainstorm turned the roads and fields into a sea of mud. It took the General over 4 hours to ride from the front to the back of the caravan of the wounded. The Colonel was absolutely correct on this little-known fact concerning the battle!

I was having a hard time grasping the fact that the Colonel and his men were in a dimension that did not realize they had passed from their incarnate lives. I asked if he was at the end of the tunnel, referring to the tunnel that leads to the light of Heaven. His answer was:

No, I am in the rear of the column.

My next question inquired if he was retreating from Gettysburg. He replied:

Yes, we are on the move.

There was no doubt that the spirit with whom we were communicating was still carrying out the orders of General Lee.

As we were finishing the previous message, it was as if all the neighbors began putting off their fireworks at once. It resembled the sound of far-off cannon fire. The pointer began to move rapidly as it spelled out the message:

Yanks surrounding us. Gunfire all around. Utter shock.

The Colonel was in a panic for the safety of his men. I tried to explain that it was not cannon fire, but the sound of people celebrating the birth of our nation with fireworks. His men were not in danger from the cannon-like noise. The Colonel seemed to calm down as a result of my explanation.

Next I asked a very direct question: "Do you know you have passed?" His reply came as no surprise:

I do not.

Now, my curiosity was fully aroused and I inquired if he believed in ghosts. His answer was a firm:

No.

We were receiving messages from a ghost that did not believe in ghosts! I then asked if he believed in an afterlife, to which he answered:

I believe in Heaven.

At this point of the session, I felt it might be a good idea to change the subject. I inquired if his men were with him, to which he answered:

Most are.

Getting back to the not knowing he passed thing, my next question was: "Are we your first contact on this side?" His answer was:

What side are you on?

[Meaning Yankee or Rebel.]
The spirit was not about to be accused of conspiring with the enemy.
Barbara Lee asked if he would pose for a picture. His reply was:

We are here for the night in the woods line.

There was a woods line along a small creek, about 200 yards from our picnic area. This would have been a perfect spot to spend the night if you were protecting a retreating column of men. If I was going to get a picture, we would have to inspire confidence with the Rebel fighter. I informed the colonel that we were friendly to the southern cause and that we were even flying the Confederate flag. He replied:

I will come with some of my men. Can you insure we will not come under fire?

As I looked around the table, I felt quite comfortable that no one in our group would fire on them, especially Connie, who was armed only with a pen. We assured them that they would be safe. His next reply was:

Thank you.

Then posed the question:

Are you from the south?

Again, he was assured that our group favored the South and that was why we were flying the southern flag. The colonel's final response to us was:

I am coming up now. I can see it. I will stand by the flag.

With that response, Barbara Lee and I headed for the area of the flag with cameras in hand.

Barbara Lee's husband has constructed a fort-like structure on their property from which he can observe the abundant wildlife in the area. The flag pole flying the Confederate flag stands next to the structure, giving it an almost fort-like appearance, much like the Civil War structures. As soon as Barbara Lee approached the area of the flag, she commented that she could sense the soldiers around her. She told the soldiers that they would be safe and could feel free to spend the night in the structure if they wished. While she was speaking to them, I was busy snapping pictures.

Upon reviewing the photographs of the evening, there were several that proved the presence of the Southern spirits on that July night. In one of the most memorable photos (shown on this page), a bright orb

A spirit orb passes in front of the Confederate flag on the 4th of July. Note the flag is being blown in one direction and the orb is moving into the wind.

A Rebel soldier, still fighting the Civil War, stares at the Stars and Bars of the Confederacy.

is moving rapidly passed the Confederate flag. The camera was set to 1/200 of a second to give you an idea of how fast the orb was moving. Pay special attention to the fact that the wind was blowing the flag in one direction and the orb was moving against the wind.

In another photograph taken at a different angle, you can see the distinct image of a Confederate soldier in the window of the structure looking directly at the flag. This is probably the first time the soldiers looked at a real flag for 149 years.

If you look on the right side of the flag pole through the window, you will see a faint shape of a face. The soldier's eyes, nose, and mouth are visible as he looks at the flag. There is no glass in the window so reflection is not a possibility.

Since the soldiers seemed to feel safe and secure for the night, we now left them alone and returned to the marguerites. Hopefully, we will be able to contact them again next year during the 150th anniversary of the battle. I know we will definitely fly the Stars and Bars again next year.

The forms of soldiers still fighting the Battle of Gettysburg are photographed in the Wheat Field.

Afterlife: What Really Happens on the Other Side

The concept that ghost soldiers are still fighting on the battlefield is not a new one. I have been with clairvoyants who can still hear the sounds of fighting such as commands to fire and charge. We have recorded the sound of cannon fire, but thought it was residual haunting. Perhaps it was the sound of continued fighting. Barbara Lee has had experiences where the spirits with whom she was channeling offered to escort her to a safer place.

Many of my pictures show ectoplasm forms that have the appearance of continued fighting. In my photographs of the battlefield, there have been other examples of soldiers still fighting, but it never occurred to me that they might not be aware they had passed from the life plane. In the photograph of ectoplasm forms on the previous page taken on the Wheat Field at Gettysburg, you can see that the soldiers seem to still be fighting.

Neither Barbara Lee nor I had ever encountered a situation where we were dealing with ghosts that did not know they had passed. The Heavenly guides had introduced us to an entirely new dimension. How a spirit could exist without knowing it had passed, haunted (pardon the pun) me long after the July 4th session. It seems like the guides only give out enough information to assure that my quest for knowledge concerning the afterlife is unending.

While on a short vacation at my home in Utah the next month, I attended a channeling session with my friends who had introduced me to the Spirit Board. I mentioned the strange July 4th interview and they were anxious to help. My first question of the guides concerned the Confederate colonel, and this was their response:

OK, remember there are two channels. You have one to the knowing dead and one to the unknowing dead. They do not remember and we will not interfere. You and your helpers help play with both where you believe in understanding. Yes, knowing souls want to talk.

Apparently, there is a channel or dimension where the spirits really do not know that they have passed from the life plane.

The afterlife must be an amazingly complex place. There is a channel of the knowing dead and the unknowing dead. There is no time dimension. There are earthbound spirits and Heavenly Guides, whose feet have never touched the earth. All this is run by a hierarchy of saints, angels, minor gods, and major gods. Once again, the guides had given us just enough information to peak interest.

As I have had time to reflect on the session with the Confederate colonel and the subsequent message from the guides, I think the key to partial understanding lies in the last sentence: "knowing souls want to talk." This is why all of our previous sessions were with the earthbound spirits or the knowing dead. Our experience indicates that the knowing dead are more than eager to use the communication channel provided by our group.

My belief is that it was a quirk of fate that allowed us to contact the souls of the colonel and his men. It was being in the right place at the right time to coincide with the events of 149 years ago that allowed us to contact the channel of the unknowing dead. Why that channel exists, who is destined to an afterlife where they do not know they have passed, how long the soul remains in that channel, and many other questions remain unanswered.

One question that I need to remember to ask the guides is why they don't interfere with the channel of the unknowing dead and help them move on. The colonel indicated that he believed in Heaven. In spite of his belief, the Colonel, along with his men, have been destined to keep fighting for the last 149 years. My guess is that the guides have absolutely no intention of passing on any more of their secrets until they are ready to open a new door to yet another aspect of the afterlife.

Chapter 18

I Will Always be There

As a child, I grew up in a small town north of Hershey, Pennsylvania. My family operated a country store, which was the center of the rural community and first opened for business in the 1890s. My grandfather, George Schaffner, supported many of the local residents during the Great Depression by offering credit to all. Quite often, those debts would be forgiven when the families were unable to pay. He was a kind and generous person who was highly respected by all who knew him. Because of his generosity, in spite of having a successful business, he never amassed much wealth. He passed when I was only nine years old, and all my life I have regretted not being able to better know him. True to the traditions of the times, his viewing was held in the home, and I can remember a long line of neighbors coming to pay their respects. To this day, I cannot think of a finer role model.

The more I have become associated with the spirit world, the more I have thought about my grandfather. One inevitable consequence of growing old is watching the passing of your parents and grandparents. Even though I keep my grandfather's photograph on my desk along with other members of my family, my memories of him have faded since he passed sixty years ago. Recently, I have been seeing his image in my mind's eye more vividly than ever before. With Barbara Lee's help, I was about to find out a lot more about my grandfather than I ever realized.

On several occasions, the name "George" had come up on the Ghost Box, but it was difficult to get any distinct messages. It always seemed like the static would drown it out. I had thought the spirit presence leaving his name was probably my long-passed grandfather, but I couldn't be positive.

The introduction of the Spirit Board opened the door to many possibilities in our quest to communicate with the spirits on the other side of the life veil. As we learned to use the board, we began to get multiple messages from the other side. During one of the sessions, I found myself calling out the name "George." I asked the question: "Is this my grandfather?" The glass indicator went to the word "Hello." My grandfather was making an appearance on the talking board. Just to make sure, I asked him to answer "yes" if it was truly George Schaffner, my grandfather. The glass moved very rapidly to the word:

Yes.

My grandmother, also kind and generous, passed in 1960 of a cancer. My grandparents had been devoted to each other in life, so I asked the question, "Are you with Grandma?" The glass again rapidly moved to the word:

Yes.

I knew in my heart they would be together in Heaven. At that point, I inquired if he was with my other family members: I asked about my Aunt Beulah, my mother, Pauline (his two daughters, very close to them in life), and my grandfather's sister, Aunt Annie. The glass moved rapidly to "yes" for all of them. It is obvious that close family ties continue in Heaven.

I then asked if my uncle and father were with them and received no answer. These were the sons-in-law and not related by birth. This lack of answer puzzled me at the time, but I have come to the conclusion that souls tend to stay together by birth lines or soulmates in prior lives. My father has appeared several times and he is usually accompanied by spirits from his side of the family. When we get messages from my mother, she is usually with her side of the family. (I told their story in Chapter 12: Mom and Dad.)

At this point of the session, the glass pointer moved to the words "goodbye." When the spirits are tired of a conversation, they let you know it, and he was apparently finished for the evening. The events of the session had been outstanding, but it was only a harbinger of things to come!

The next day, I received a phone call from Barbara Lee. She was completely blown away by the events of the previous evening. We agreed to try the board again the next evening to verify that the events of Saturday night could be repeated. Needless to say, expectations were running very high as we prepared the Spirit Board by lubricating the surface to make the glass pointer slide as easily as possible. We were not to be disappointed!

The glass moved toward "Message for" and then spelled out "Barry." Whoever the spirit was, the message was going to be directed toward yours truly. It did not take long to find out who was coming through. The pointer spelled out the letters:

George.

My grandfather was back again to continue the conversation.

The next message scored a "10" on my emotional meter. As I watched the glass move rapidly to the letters, the message became clear. It spelled out:

Afterlife: What Really Happens on the Other Side

I am always around you.

For once in my life I was at a loss for words as the full impact of the message sunk into my thick head.

After gathering a little composure, I asked the question: "Are you also around my daughters?" To this question he answered:

Some of the time.

At least they were under his protection some of the time. I had already found out in earlier sessions that my father looks out for my daughters and granddaughters, but that is another story.

I have always been conscientious about trying to follow the wishes of the spirits. My belief is that the reason for Barbara Lee and my success is that we are attempting to follow their wishes. Next, I asked if there was anything else I could do to follow their wishes. His answer was:

Keep up the good work.

I felt very good about this vote of confidence. A compliment from your grandfather is always appreciated, especially when he passed so long ago.

The next word to be spelled on the board was:

Hunting.

As a young man, my grandfather loved to hunt. When he was only twelve years old, he was accidently shot in his upper thigh and that affected his mobility. He never talked about how he was hurt, but I was told he was accidentally injured by his brother. By the time he was in his late twenties, the injury had degenerated his leg to the point that he could only walk with an ankle brace or a cane.

The word "hunting" certainly brought back more memories. In my mind, I could see him strapping on the metal brace that allowed him to get around to wait on customers in the store. As my mind snapped back to the business at hand, the pointer spelled the word:

Cane.

He was proving beyond any doubt that the spirit of my grandfather was present with us in the room.

I asked the question: "Who else is with you?" The pointer spelled the name:

Annie.

This was my grandfather's sister, a sweet woman that I cannot remember ever uttering a swear word. I asked if she was fine. The answer on the board was:

Yes.

We had discussed his sister in our previous session, so I knew the Schaffner family circle, much like the lyrics to the song, "Family Circle" was pretty much complete.

Getting back to the board session, now the pointer gave us the name:

Billy.

I knew several Bills or Williams who had passed, but I could not figure out who Billy was. Once again, he clarified the name with a detailed answer:

Billy was my best friend as a boy; we were like brothers.

I could not remember the name. My next question was whether my cousin, Dick (my last surviving blood relative), knew Billy? The pointer moved to the word:

No.

The identity of Billy remains a mystery to both me and my cousin. We do, though, know Billy is in Heaven with my grandfather.

Now the pointer gave us:

Lucy.

I could not recognize this name. Realizing that I needed help on this one, he read my mind and answered:

Was a dog.

It seems like even the family pets are present! Next, he spelled the words:

Hunting, fishing.

I asked: "Are you still fishing?" The answer was:

Yes, but mostly hunting.

His debilitating leg injury was no longer bothering him. Heaven seems to get better and better all the time! The new word on the board was:

Cigar.

Afterlife: What Really Happens on the Other Side

I asked whether he was still smoking. The answer came back:

No.

Thanks goodness; smoking can kill you. The pointer now moved to "Good bye" ending the channeling session. Judging from the abrupt ending, my guess is I upset him by asking about his smoking.

The proof of my grandfather's presence has shown up on numerous occasions. One day, two well-known mediums from the Pittsburgh area came into the store. I took them to our room where the paranormal experience sessions are held and they became quite excited. One of them looked at me and, without knowing anything about my personal life, asked the question: "Who is George?" I replied that he was my grandfather. She mentioned that he was standing in back of me and puffing on a cigar. That caught me off-guard, I thought he had quit smoking over there. Next, the medium told me that he said: "He's a really good boy; I am proud of him." It had been a really long time since I was referred to as a boy. I guess I can forgive him for telling me he quit smoking.

Several months later, I invited my cousin to attend a channeling session. Although he is several years older, Dick and I were raised in the same house and he knew my grandfather far better than I did. My plan was to attempt a family reunion with my deceased relatives.

I started the session by asking for the spirit presence of George Schaffner. My request was immediately answered with the word:

Hello.

My guess is that our grandfather had been waiting for us. I started by saying: "Do you see who is with us tonight?" His reply was:

What took you so long, boy?

Did I mention before that my grandfather could be quite gruff and to the point? He appeared to be a little impatient that I took so long in inviting his other grandson.

Dick had brought along his daughter and son-in-law. My grandfather proceeded to say how happy he was with the way my cousin's family had led their lives. Before the session ended, we had appearances from my Aunt Beulah, Dick's mother. My mother also made an appearance to say "hello" to him.

The most memorable part of the conversation with our grandfather occurred midway through the reading. My cousin and his wife lost their first baby in childbirth over fifty years prior. Dick asked if the soul of their baby was with them in Heaven. The reply caught us all by surprise. It was:

She's back.

The glass pointer immediately spelled out:

We were not supposed to say that.

We had just received confirmation of reincarnation from a spirit I really trusted, my grandfather! No matter how I tried with follow-up questions, he would not say any more about the slip of his spirit tongue. After the session, we all discussed the possibility that she might have come back as one of their current grandchildren. As I have said many times in this book, soul families stick together through time.

As I consider the large amount of information that has come from my grandfather during the various channeling and Ghost Box sessions, I know I am blessed with being reunited with his spirit. The words that keep being repeated in my head are: "I'll always be around you." It is amazing how much comfort you can find in five words.

Understanding Reincarnation

Your soul has a family group that stays together through time and your soul relationship will vary through different reincarnations. For example, you might be husband and wife in this lifetime, but brother and sister in the prior. When I asked the guide how many lifetimes my wife and I have been together, he replied: "6 or 7."

- The decision to return or reincarnate is made by the individual soul. As you read in Chapter 10, the soul of Ulysses Grant has made a decision to return, but his wife, Julia, will not return with him.
- A main reason for reincarnation is soul experience. The more the soul learns, the more it advances on the other side.
- New souls are not created. As population increases, people reincarnate more rapidly.
- Your soul family will generally wait to reincarnate until their generation of incarnate lives have passed. The souls of the deceased will continue to help protect the lives of those remaining.
- Your soul family may actually act as guardian angels, helping you in time of need.
- It is possible for souls to make the decision to marry while on the other side, before reincarnating.
- After birth, the soul has free will to make its decisions on how they will spend their lifetime.
- The time of death is preordained while on the other side. Deceased souls continually tell us "it was my time."
- The decision for evil is never made on the other side. It is a decision made after birth.

Chapter 19

A Young Girl with an Old Soul

Throughout my life I have met some very impressive and memorable individuals. This story is about a very memorable person who happens to be a nine-year-old girl. As I become more heavily involved with the paranormal, I am more fascinated with clairvoyance and reincarnation. My belief is that the soul becomes more astute as it learns from life experiences during the numerous periods in the plane of human life. As the soul ages, I believe it becomes more in touch with the spirit world. An old soul will have amazing abilities and knowledge having learned from many prior life mistakes.

As we hold the sessions at Golden Lane, our guests witness amazing examples of clairvoyance from Barbara Lee. I have no doubt that Barbara's soul has been around for quite awhile and has paid very close attention during her various lifetimes. She has been an immense help in my understanding of what really takes place around us.

For several months, I had been hearing about a young girl named Noelle who talked about her spirit playmates and actually had conversations with fairies and other supernatural beings. My curiosity was aroused and I attempted to have the girl and her mother come to the store and see how she responded to our spirit population. Unfortunately, we could never work out a satisfactory schedule.

One day, in the summer of 2011, my phone rang and it was Noelle's mother, also a clairvoyant, to tell me that they could come to the store for a visit. I was elated at the opportunity of meeting the young girl in person and asking her questions about our spirits. I made a point of not mentioning any names or giving any information about our resident ghosts.

Noelle and her mother arrived at the store just before closing time. We left the lights on, so that they could visit all the areas of the store at their leisure. As I was introduced to the young lady and we began to talk, I was impressed by her maturity. She spoke like she was nine years old going on twenty-one. As I was to find out, Noelle truly communicated on a higher plane and reflected a maturity beyond her years. At times during the visit, it was as if I was communicating with a Spirit Guide without the talking board.

Noelle and her mother began the tour of the store by walking down several of the aisles without any direction or clues about our spirit friends. They walked into a booth holding a large oil painting that we knew from experience was haunted by an unhappy spirit. Noelle expressed heaviness and a feeling of sadness. Without any help, she reinforced what we had been told by other clairvoyants about the oil painting.

We all went upstairs and began to walk around the long aisles filled with antiques. After a while we could not find Noelle and I called out her name. We could hear her voice from a far back corner of the store. As I walked to the booth where her voice was coming from, I suddenly became aware of her lying on the floor, playing with a spinning wheel.

New Friends

She said: "Hi, I am playing with my new friend, Jenny. She likes the spinning wheel."

The only person I could see in the booth was Noelle. Every time I think I know most of the ghosts in the building, a new one makes its presence felt. We had not heard the name Jenny before. I asked if that was her new friend's spinning wheel. Noelle replied that Jenny only liked to play with it. This young girl lived in a world where conversations with spirits were a regular and common activity. I suggested she tell Jenny to come downstairs with us where we had the cameras so we could see her and talk to her on the Ghost Box.

Orbs are photographed in the viewing room at Golden Lane Antique Gallery.

Our viewing room at Golden Lane is equipped with special cameras and large screen television sets that allow us to view the movement of orbs and shadow figures in real time. It is also where we use our Ghost Box to hear spirit responses in live time. I was very anxious to watch the activity that Noelle would bring to the viewing room. As we turned off the overhead lights and the special cameras came on, I was not disappointed as the room became full of moving orbs. The nine year old was the equivalent of an orb magnet. A large orb slowly circled in front of the camera. Noelle simply said: "That's Jenny." Apparently, the newfound friend followed her to the lower level of the building. With all the orb activity going on around us, I got out the Ghost Box and turned it on. When we attempted to make contact with Jenny, we could hear the faint voice of a little girl. Unfortunately, her answers were too weak to understand.

As the Ghost Box continued emitting its steady background sound, a large, disk-like orb passed slowly in front of the camera. Noelle proudly announced: "That's Dave." Her mother promptly replied that she thought she had told Noelle to leave Dave at home. The young girl responded that she knew it was not polite to invite a ghost to another person's home, but she told Dave it was okay to come along with her tonight because he helps watch over her. Not only did I learn something about ghost etiquette, but it seemed that Dave thought a road trip was a good idea.

I now asked Dave to say "hello" if he was present. We all heard a very clear male voice say: "Hello." Not only had Noelle's ghost friend accompanied her to the store, he was in a talkative mood. Everyone in the room joined in saying "hi" back to Dave in unison. This was clearly not a place for nonbelievers.

In an effort to learn more about our visiting ghost, I asked him if he had a last name. There was a male reply, but it was difficult to understand against the static of the Ghost Box. I asked him to repeat the name and this time you could make out "Bine." The name of our visitor was Dave Bine. (I later verified the name when I reviewed the tapes.) Next, I asked Dave his age. Noelle immediately interjected: "He's twenty-two years old." I rephrased the question to: "Are you twenty-two years old?" and the answer came back: "Yes." Our visitor was just over voting age when he passed. She now asked Dave to pass slowly in front of the cameras and a large orb made an appearance on the screen. It was becoming more obvious that Noelle had detailed conversations with her spirit friends and everything she told us was being verified over the Ghost Box. We were witnessing a rare and amazing supernatural ability in a nine-year-old girl.

Fairies

Over the past several years, I have taken thousands of paranormal pictures. I have *not* been able to identify many of the images, as I have captured subjects that are truly

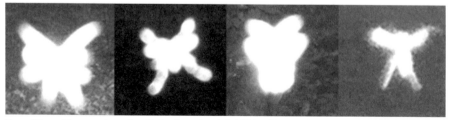

Four different images from the Gettysburg battlefield identified as fairies by Noelle.

unusual. In fact, a portion of our introductory session is entitled: "The Unknown." This was a golden opportunity to have our young guest look at the pictures to see if she could identify them. As I put one of the images on the large screen, she immediately answered in a tone that implied everyone in the room should have known what we were observing: "That's a fairy." We received the same reply for the next three pictures.

She then began to expand on the fairies' personal appearances by saying that the only thing they really get right in the movies is that fairies have pointed ears. And, by the way, they are vegetarians and not carnivores. Not only did the young lady have running conversations with ghosts, she played with fairies on a regular basis and even knew their eating habits.

Jeff Again!

While sitting in the room, Noelle mentioned that there was a man by the name of Jeff standing in the corner. She said he kept repeating his name. I told her it was Jeff Silverman, an old friend of ours that used to work in the building when it was a shoe factory. I advised her that he was also our most dependable spirit when it came to talking on the Ghost Box.

As part of our paranormal experience, I run a video segment showing a large orb come out of the wall, move toward the camera, and then circle back through the room. When I run it in slow motion, you can see the eyes of the orb looking at the camera. As Noelle viewed the video clip, she said: "That's Jeff." She recognized my spirit friend from his orb presence.

From an earlier session, we have a video of a shadow figure looking into one of our cameras. Last week, I caught a glimpse of a shadow figure in the back of the room. The guest sitting next to me also saw it at the same time, verifying that I was not hallucinating. Noelle now made the statement that a black shadow person kept looking around the curtains in the back of the room. She said he was too bashful to come into the room with our group. Another mystery was solved! When the session ended, I realized the evening had provided a lot of information for a chapter in my next book.

Other "Beings"

I did not see Noelle again until June of 2012. We had been working with the Spirit Board and I was curious to see if her natural metaphysical abilities would allow her to channel and bring us more detailed messages. As I was to find out, not only could she and her mother get messages from souls on the other side, we were about to hear from the souls of subjects that were not human beings when in an incarnate form. If you think some of the other happenings in this book are weird, buckle up. There are four witnesses to what took place and can vouch for the facts.

In my readings concerning the spiritual world, I ran across articles that stated the soul can return in various forms, not necessarily human. In my own mind, I rejected the idea that a soul would ever want to return as an animal or maybe even a tree as part of the reincarnation and learning process. I also read that animals have souls and spirits similar to humans. My first book includes several photographs of ghost dogs, so I knew they definitely had spirits. I wasn't sure they had souls.

As the session with Noelle began, we were having trouble getting responses on the Spirit Board. We tried various combinations and finally decided to try three persons on the glass at the same time. Noelle, her mother Marion, and I put our fingers on the glass pointer. Our combined energies began to get results and Marion's father came through and gave her some advice. Her deceased Dad strongly advised the young girl's mother to quit smoking. Noelle agreed. We were finally starting to get definitive results.

Noelle stated that she was always surrounded by animal spirits and asked if she could try to talk to them. She asked the question: "Is Cup Cake (her deceased cat) here?" To my amazement, the pointer spelled out:

Yes, I love you.

If the Spirit Guides were messing with us, they were doing one heck of a job! I looked at Noelle and the expression on her face was that talking to her animal friends was business as usual.

She then asked whether Chabella was there. The pointer then spelled out:

Yes, I too love you.

I could not resist asking her who Chabella was. She explained that it was her dead hamster. I almost choked at the idea of communicating with a dead hamster. Noelle then asked how Chabella was doing. The pointer spelled out the word:

Happy.

As I looked around the room at the faces of the adults present, I could tell they were contemplating the thought of a happy hamster in Heaven.

Just when I thought it couldn't get much more bizarre, Noelle asked if Buddha was there. The pointer spelled out:

Yes, sorry.

I inquired as to the identity of Buddha and she answered that this was her dog. My next question was why was Buddha, the dog, sorry? Marion explained that Buddha had killed the hamster. At this point, I was thinking about where I hid the Irish whiskey! Not only do animals have souls that can communicate with us, they can apologize for what they did in life. She then tried to reach her dead goldfish. I was very happy when we didn't get a reply and I breathed a sigh of relief. I could not have handled getting a message from a goldfish.

Noelle was now quite excited at the prospect of communicating with all her former pets. She made a last attempt at contacting her pet rabbit, Chloe. When she asked the question about whether Chloe was there, the answer was:

Yes, been waiting for you.

When Noelle asked where, the answer was:

New life, 2013.

She then asked if Chloe was going to be a bunny and the answer was:

Don't know.

As hard as it is to believe, the message indicated that the soul of her pet rabbit was going to return to her in the year 2013 in an undisclosed form. (Remember, this session was held in 2012.) It was obvious that her deceased pets shared the love that she felt for them.

Other Perspectives

After the session and the impact of what had just taken place sunk in, I became troubled by the thought of having direct contact with animals. After discussing the event with Barbara Lee, I felt there was a distinct possibility that an evil spirit could have given us false information. Barbara Lee has almost fifty years of metaphysical experience and strongly cautioned against the concept of direct communications with animals. She stated that animals had their separate areas in Heaven and messages could not be given directly.

I contacted my friends at the Ray of Light in Salt Lake City and asked them if they had any experience with direct contact from animals. K and Laurie were quick to respond. In the forty years they have been channeling with the Spirit Guides, there has been a long history of animals returning to their loved ones. Animals have souls and spirits. Upon passing, the soul returns to Heaven and can communicate through the Spirit Guides, much like the human soul.

Another statement from my friends also caught me by surprise! Animals are often a person's guide who wants to live a life with their human. Noelle is constantly surrounded by the spirits of animals. The thought that her guides would like to accompany such a compassionate girl through life seems to be a distinct possibility. Maybe her pet rabbit was really a guide that enjoyed the visit so much, it will be joining her again in the year 2013. If my daughters read this chapter, they will surely have me committed.

Afterlife: What Really Happens on the Other Side

In subsequent conversations with Noelle's mother, I have come to understand that Noelle's perspective on relationships and interactions often comes from a higher place. Her exposure to a different point of view gives her a kind of wisdom that is uncommon. She tends to see the emotion behind the statement, the intention behind the action, the desire, fear, and pain behind the event, and, as such, she responds in ways that are insightful and compassionate. She is often fearless of and frequently oblivious to much of the nonsense we walk through in our everyday lives. In essence, her maturity comes from an ability to see the "greater" picture.

I find it very hard to visualize the incredible world that Noelle must see through her mind's eye. If the soul advances toward spiritual understanding and visualization with each visit to the human plane, the spiritual age of our "young" old soul must be very great indeed. Her soul has undoubtedly been on the earth many times in the past.

Chapter 20

Death:
The Beginning,
Not The End

Death is defined as an event that occurs when all biological functions that sustain a living organism come to a halt. From all causes, roughly 150,000 people die around the world each day. In the clinical definition of death, there is no mention of the spiritual aspects of dying. Nonbelievers in the spiritual aspects of life see all things ending at the time of death.

Classic religions believe in the existence of the soul. According to their teachings, if you follow the rules of "the good book," the soul will pass into Heaven where it will reside for eternity. If you failed to follow the rules, you will go to a place that is hot and nasty. I was never sure what happened if you were on the dividing line and who made the decision as to which direction your soul was dispatched.

We have heard messages from the other side that say the church has a lot to learn and that Heaven is not what the spirit expects. When we attempt to delve deeper into the details of what Heaven is really like, we don't receive any additional answers. There are definitely certain details that you will have to die to find out.

I have discussed the concept of reincarnation on many occasions in this book. Belief in the concept of an incarnate rebirth is fundamental to the assumptions of this chapter. Since dying is the logical starting point for the departure to the afterlife, I thought it might be interesting to delve into what happens when you die.

As we become more familiar with the spirit world and our communications with the guides become more complex, the act of dying becomes a regular topic of conversation. In my humble opinion, the incarnate life ends with death, as the soul and spirit leave the physical body and begin a journey that will culminate in a reincarnation that launches another incarnate life experience. The true mystery is what happens between the death and the reincarnate birth.

At the time of passing, tests have shown that the body actually loses weight as the spirit and soul depart the corpse. I have clairvoyant friends who have heard the sound of the soul departing the body at time of death. Nurses who work in hospice also tell of the phenomenon. Apparently, the soul is so anxious to get on with its new experience that it rushes out of the body.

What happens when the individual dies has haunted humanity since the beginning of time. Our experience is that the Spirit Board utilized by a clairvoyant provides the most detailed information from the deceased. This opinion seems to be backed up by thousands of years of experience.

Preordained Death

In order for the recently departed to communicate, a Heavenly guide is required to provide the channel or energy source. There are guides for deceased souls that assist the earthbound spirits in getting their messages through to the living. We have had guests request a spirit presence and the guide has spelled out the word: "wait." In a couple of minutes, the requested spirit shows up and communication begins on the Spirit Board. Once again, there seems to be a really efficient paging system on the other side.

Carol Green, in her book *You and Your Board of Guides,* records transcripts gathered from over forty years of communicating with the Heavenly guides and departed souls. In one of her sessions, the question was asked: "Please explain death to us?" The answer was: "Death is only a rebirth into Heaven. As life is made, so it is taken. This is the law that is never broken." Another statement that I find quite profound is: "Dying is simple. It is the living that is hard." The Spirit Guides view death as only one step in the process of the chain of life.

Our experience indicates that the time of death is actually preordained. There are occasions where a near-death occurrence happens, when there is a traumatic event that causes the body to stop functioning for a short period of time. The spirit may leave the body, but I believe the soul remains. Many people have heard of the events that take place for persons with a near-death experience (NDE). Some describe floating above their bodies and actually observing the events taking place around their incarnate bodies. Others describe a tunnel with a light at the end. They all describe a feeling of unbelievable peace and tranquility.

We have a friend whose heart stopped beating on the operating table during surgery. She remembers looking down on the doctors frantically working to save her life. While observing the events taking place below, she experienced a feeling of well being and sensed no pain. When the doctors hit her the third time with the electric paddles, she suffered excruciating pain as the spirit reentered her body as though on a sliding board.

Upon awakening, she recounted her memory of what she had observed. The doctors confirmed that they had indeed used the paddles on three different occasions. There was no way she could have known the details of how the doctors brought her back to life. Her spirit had actually observed the activity in the operating room, but it was not time for her soul to leave the life plane. It simply was not her time.

We have also found that dislike and hatred can pass into the afterlife. If an individual did not like someone in life, it seems as though the relationship does not improve much in the next dimension. We had contact with an individual that had been unhappy in his marriage and had told his wife he wanted a divorce shortly before his passing. Upon his death, the widow carried out none of his wishes and did not even attend the funeral. In our session on the Spirit Board with the individual, we learned that he still despised his wife, now almost sixty years since his passing. The spirit had observed the misdeeds of his wife and the emotions had become even more inflamed as the years passed since his death. When the wife passes, I can imagine there will be sparks at the end of the tunnel!

In Chapter 13, I told of our session with Ulysses Grant. In life, he and George Custer had a very strong dislike for each other. When I asked him what he thought of Custer his answer was: "Custer was a damn fool." I would take it from that answer that the act of dying does little to settle old differences.

One evening, during one of our Ghost Box sessions, we heard proof that spirits can actually argue with each other on the other side. As we were listening closely for messages, everyone in the room heard a clear: "Your mother, asshole." This was not exactly what I was expecting. Barbara Lee responded by scolding the spirit and telling him that this type of language was not acceptable. When I went back and listened to the tape, I discovered that the nasty response had been triggered by another comment. One spirit had called the other "asshole" and the other had replied: "Your mother, asshole." For those of you who don't believe this type of interaction can happen, I have the audio posted on my web site, www.ghostsofgoldenlane.com for you to hear. Death does not seem to have slowed up the argument between these two spirits.

Many sources of evidence reinforce the idea that an individual's time of death is preordained. Carol Green's book also addresses this issue when she asked the guides the question: "Is there ever such a thing as an accidental death that was not in the plan for life?" The answer was: "Yes, but very, very, very, very, very, very few die suddenly or unplanned." Souls seem to have some control over their future life plan. This makes sense if you believe that soulmates stay together through successive times on earth.

Several months ago, an acquaintance of Barbara Lee passed suddenly. There had been some discussion in the newspapers that more could have been done to save his life. When we asked the Spirit Guides if his life could have been saved, we received the answer:

It was his time.

Apparently, when it is time to pass, there is nothing here on earth that will change the preordained life plan.

Unexpected Death

Another reoccurring theme that we have learned from our sessions is that when an individual dies suddenly in an accident, the soul is completely surprised to find out it is on the other side of the life veil. We contacted a close friend of Barbara Lee who had been taken suddenly in an automobile accident. When we made contact, it had been less than a week since his passing. Barbara asked the question as to how he was doing on the other side. His reply was:

At first, it really freaked me out when I realized where I was.

His soul was as surprised at his sudden passing as everyone who knew him on earth. He then went on to say that everything was now fine.

When the individual undergoes a sudden and unexpected death, the soul often has regrets that he or she did not get the opportunity to say goodbye to their love ones. Barbara's previously discussed friend spent much of the session giving her specific messages of love to give to his surviving family members and friends. Unfinished business is a major reason for a soul to remain earthbound as it attempts to complete its mission. Many of the messages we get on the Spirit Board are earthbound souls attempting to pass messages of love and continuing devotion to those remaining on the earth plane. They may simply remain behind to help the loved one when his or her time comes to pass over.

Helping Others Cross Over

At one of our sessions, we had two guests whose mother was in very poor health in a nursing home. Contact was made with the deceased sister of the guests' mother. Her message was that she had returned to help with the passing of the mother in the nursing home. Two days later, our customer called to say that his mother had passed, but that the knowledge that her passing was made easier by the presence of his aunt who gave him great comfort.

Davy Jones of the music group The Monkees passed away suddenly in February 2012 of a massive heart attack while in Florida. One evening, he made his appearance while we were conducting a channeling session. His first message was:

I was not prepared to go.

When we asked if he was upset, the answer was:

Very.

When we asked if there was anything we could do to help, his answer was:

Pray for me.

Barbara asked if there was anything that could have been done to save his life and the answer from the guide was:

It was his time.

This shows that there can be some very troubled souls on the other side, and I believe that the first item of business before moving on is to find peace within their own souls and to accept what has happened.

Taking Your Own Life

When you die a natural death, the guides say you encounter the tunnel and loved ones to help your soul adapt to the new surroundings. What happens when you commit suicide and take your own life? Carol Green's book once again sheds some light on this. The guide addressed what happens when an individual commits suicide:

- When you die, you are at peace with Heaven and earth. When killing one's self, the hatred grabs at you. It is as if you are falling downward, uncontrollably downward in the darkness, and all unfinished things are grabbing at you, trying to bring you back to complete them. And the people who should have been, and those who have been, grab at you. Then nothing: darkness, silence, and emptiness.

The question was asked if the unlived parts of a life are lost forever.

- No, the lessons not lived will be completed, so you do not fix anything. Plus, you must live your mistake over from all kinds of ways.

In another quote, the spirit of the actual person committing suicide is quoted:

- As I died, I saw the kids that I never had, the strings never tied, all the lessons never learned. I will not do it again for sure. It muffs up too many lives for me to be responsible for. I now must make it up to a lot of souls.

It appears the penalties for committing suicide are many, from being sent to a dark and empty part of Heaven, to making it up to all the souls left behind who were hurt by your actions. We have tried on numerous occasions to contact individuals who had committed suicide and the guides have not allowed them to make contact through the Spirit Board. If persons contemplating suicide think they have it bad on this side, they should consider the fact that they may have it worse on the other side.

If there is one reality for the living, it is the fact that we will all face the inevitability of death. Personally, I am quite comfortable with the concept that death is just the beginning, not the end. However, as I am finishing up this chapter, the words of the Kenney Chesney song comes to mind: "Everybody wants to go to Heaven, but nobody wants to go now." I am also aware that when that time comes, there is no action that will alter my preordained plan of life. For my spirit, soul, and soulmates, death will begin another journey and incredible adventure.

Suicide is NOT the Answer

A special note to any reader that might be contemplating suicide:

You will have a soul experience after this lifetime. If you do not believe in an afterlife, you will be in for a rude awakening when you die.

As you can see from the exact words of those who have killed themselves and the words of the guides in this chapter, death will NOT be the end of your suffering. Your soul will have to watch the suffering of all the living individuals who you leave behind. Instead of finding peace, your soul goes to a place of darkness and emptiness. All suicide does is create misery and suffering for the living.

If you are contemplating suicide, get help!

Here are a few suggestions:

• Read This First: www.metanoia.org/suicide/.
• National Suicide Prevention Hotline: www.suicidepreventionlifeline.org/.
• American Foundation for Suicide Prevention: www.afsp.org/.

Chapter 21

Death Has its Perks

When I first started to write this story, we had been holding our paranormal sessions at Golden Lane Antique Gallery for over a year. Some of our earliest guests were three women from the Washington, D.C. area. About every three months they would attend our sessions and became friends as well as clients. The ladies even brought other family members to see the actual paranormal activities that took place at our events. At that time, we were only using the Ghost Box to communicate with the other side.

The families of Laura, Cheryl, and Kathey lived in adjoining homes and had become very close through the years—as close as sisters. The oldest member of the group, Kathey, had a great sense of humor and enjoyed all of our events, especially the Ghost Box where she could hear the voices of the spirits in real time. She was a heavy smoker and whenever we took a break would go outside and enjoy a cigarette.

I saw her in November 2012 and I thought she did not look well. She had developed a bad cough and we actually had trouble hearing the Ghost Box because of her coughing. The last time Kathey attended one of our sessions, she had been in failing health. Since I had met her she'd had a coughing problem, but it had worsened considerably and I'd noticed she had lost weight.

Apparently, the cough was much worse than I realized. When she finally saw a doctor in December, it was too late, and cancer had damaged her body beyond repair. About four months later, Connie and I received word that she had passed. I told Connie at the time that I believed that we had not heard the last of Kathey. This was definitely a prediction that would come true.

I received an email that her two friends, Laura and Cheryl, wanted to attend a channeling session in late June. Barbara and I had only been using the Spirit Board since April of 2012. This would be the first time the ladies tried direct channeling. In the back of my mind, I thought we would have a good chance to reunite the three friends. We often find it difficult to get messages from the recently departed spirits. It seems as though they have to become accustomed to their new surroundings and learn how to use their new found energies. I also believed that if anyone could do it, Kathey could.

Kathey Arrives

Knowing this would in all probability be a special session, I limited the group size to only the two friends. Barbara Lee also knew Kathey from our previous experiences. She and I sat at the board, performed our prayer that no evil would come forward, and put our fingers on the glass. We began the channeling session by asking if there was a Spirit Guide that had a message for us.

Almost immediately the glass pointer began to spell out the name:

Raj.

He explained that he was from India and would help us on this night with our messages. Earthbound spirits require the help of a Spirit Guide to bring messages to the living. They are the guides for deceased souls and act as gatekeepers. The guide actually spells out the words for the earthbound spirits. On this evening, Raj proved to be very good at his job. His next message was what I was waiting for. Raj spelled out:

We have a lady here and she says her name is Kathey.

Our old friend got right to the point:

*Hello girls; I am doing great and no
more smoking—what a way to quit.*

I knew that of all the ways to quit a bad habit, dying is always the most effective, permanent way. Then she went on to say:

*Still adjusting. I still can't believe I'm here and that
there really is such a place. I miss you too.*

Laura mentioned that she and her young granddaughter, Haylee, still look for her, the child not fully understanding the finality of her leaving. In the past, they would sit on Kathey's porch in the evenings and the child would play with her departed friend. The pointer spelled out:

I miss her too. Give a kiss and a hug.

Laura said that when it was time to leave, Kathey would always ask for a kiss and a hug. By now, both of the friends at the table had tears running down their faces. (I made a mental note to get a box of Kleenex® for the next session.) Her next words were meant to console her friends:

Chapter 21: Death Has its Perks

Don't cry, be happy. There is no pain here.

She could clearly observe what was taking place in the room. Her words did little to end the need for a box of Kleenex.

Since Kathey's passing, there had been some strange events taking place at the homes of Laura and Cheryl. Items have been moved, pictures turned over, and strange noises could be heard. Cheryl asked if her friend had been in her house and was responsible for the mystery events. Her answer was:

I didn't go too far. I drop by. Yes, I have my ways, ha, ha, ha.

My wife, Connie, decided it was time to enter the conversation, so she asked Kathey how it felt to attend one of our sessions without having to pay. Her answer was:

Being here, it has its perks.

I had heard that people were dying to attend our sessions, but this was taking it to the extreme. (I know; that was a bad joke.)

In life, Kathey liked—no change that to *really liked*—an occasional rum and coke. Cheryl asked if there were any rum and cokes in Heaven. This question got my attention, as I was going to inquire about Irish whiskey in Heaven. My hopes were shattered by her answer.

What, are you kidding? Everyone is on a diet here; there is no food.

On a personal note, I assume that also means no Irish whiskey.

One of her friends then posed the question whether Heaven was what she expected. Her answer was:

Not sure what I was expecting. It's not what you learn about.

Kathey was a devout Catholic and her next statement surprised everyone in the room.

The church has a lot to learn.

Laura asked if she was going to help the church learn and the answer was:

No.

At that point, I thought it would be best to change the subject. This is not the first time we have heard that Heaven is not exactly what one learns about in the teachings of organized religions.

From our conversations before the session, I knew that Laura and Cheryl had some unfinished business to discuss with some other deceased family members. One of them asked the question if there were any other spirits that Kathey recognized.

There are quite a few here, but not sure who they are.

It was asked: "Did you say there are many there?" The reply was:

Yes.

It seems as though a group of spirits will gather in hopes of delivering messages to the living whenever we are using the Ghost Box or Spirit Board. Raj was determining who was allowed to deliver messages. Apparently, Kathey had figured out how to get to the front of the line.

Cheryl asked if Michael, her deceased former husband and father of her two children, was there. She replied:

Not sure, I will ask.

I guess she asked the Spirit Guide or gatekeeper and found that Michael was not present. Our experience indicates that things are very well organized up there. One of the friends then asked if she had seen Tony, Laura's deceased son-in-law, to which Kathey replied:

He is fine and sends love and congrats.

Our spirit friend had found at least one person she recognized. Laura's daughter, Melissa, had gotten married a few months earlier in a destination marriage in Aruba. Kathey had passed a month before the wedding. Laura asked if the congratulations were for Melissa's marriage. Her next answer pleased everyone.

Yes, I was there—wouldn't miss it. Not even dying stops me.

Our departed friend had indeed attended the marriage in Aruba giving new meaning to being there in spirit only.

I could not help but think back to when my daughter got married and feeling bad at the time that my father had passed twenty-two years earlier. Just before he passed, I have a vivid memory of my father and three-year-old daughter having a tea party. My guess is that he, too, had attended the wedding of my daughter and probably attended the birth of my granddaughters. If you recall, I know from getting messages from him on the Spirit Board that he continues to watch over and help protect all my girls.

As a devout Catholic, Kathey had a large collection of rosaries at her home. Laura now asked if she could have one of the rosaries. The spirit answered:

Yes, take it.

Cheryl inquired if she could have a ceramic bird from her collection. The glass pointer now spelled out:

Take what you like if there are any left.

Our friendly spirit was as generous in death as she was in life. She then said:

I will keep giving signs when I am around, ha, ha, ha.

The bond of the three ladies was not going to end anytime soon.
As we sat in silence, the glass pointer suddenly began to move rapidly.

Do what you have to. I am still alive. Please tell them for me. I love and miss you all. Take care ladies. You were and are like sisters to me. God bless you all. Bye for now.

Her spirit that left her body was clearly alive and well in a better place. That was the last we heard from Kathey that evening. The ladies' old friend had given the assurance that she was still with them and probably would be until the three would be reunited in the same dimension. In the back of my mind, I felt this would not be the last we would have contact with our old friend.

A New Session

In June 2013, Laura and Cheryl decided to attend another channeling session. This time, Laura brought along her son, who had recently gotten married. When we started the session, I asked if the spirit of Kathey was present. We received an immediate:

Yes, it is really something over here.

It seems like not much has changed in the year since we last spoke.
Laura asked if she had attended the wedding of her son and daughter-in-law. Somehow, I could have predicted the answer.

Yes, I still hang out with them.

In the back of my mind I could not help hoping she wasn't with the newlyweds all the time. The next inquiry asked whether she'd danced at the wedding and the reply was:

Yes.

When asked if she had a drink, the answer was:

Naw.

It would seem that she is still missing her rum and cokes.

Kathey's house is still standing vacant and Laura helps care for it. She mentioned that whenever passing by the home, she still expects to see her departed friend looking out the window. The spirit replied:

Thank you for looking after the place.
You just might see if you look hard enough.

A final question inquired whether she was still flirting in Heaven. Her reply was:

Who cares. It was fun. We had good times.

Even in death, the ladies still seem to have fun.

As we were leaving the building that night, our guests were inquiring when they would be able to attend another session and continue the conversation with their old friend. I am sure Kathey is also waiting for the next time Laura and Cheryl come to town, especially since she has learned to get to the front of the spirit line.

Death certainly does have its perks.

Chapter 22

Hell, Satan, Lucifer, and Heaven

While doing research for this book, I encountered a quote that I thought was quite relevant.

> *Dying is like getting audited by the IRS...something that*
> *only happens to other people...until it happens to you.*
> *~Jerome P. Crabb*

Throughout the ages, man has attempted to figure out what to do when the tax man calls and what happens after death—maybe not in that specific order. Organized religions focused on the concept that the good would go to Heaven and the "bad" would go to Hell. The classic version of Hell included a perpetual fire where the soul would reside forever, much like a toasted marshmallow that catches fire and you can't seem to blow it out. In addition to the fire, the Devil, with horns and a red suit, would run around and stab the soul of sinners with a pitch fork, probably in the butt.

Historically, this unsavory picture of damnation provided all the incentive needed for church members to stay on the straight and narrow. It also gave preachers the ability to hold the threat of Hell and the Devil over the heads of parishioners, like the sword of Damocles. I was always confused why the main reason to pursue a loving God was because of the fear of Hell. Something just did not seem right about that.

When you come into our store, we have signs describing our channeling sessions. Whenever Barbara Lee and I use the Spirit Board to communicate with the spirits of deceased family members of our guests, we refer to the program as "Lifting the Veil." Occasionally, a customer will come in, take one look at our signs, and inform me that I am going straight to Hell for communicating with the dead. I don't have the heart to tell them that I don't believe there is a Hell to go straight to.

Next, they will generally say what we do is evil and the Bible is very clear about not messing with the dead. Generally, these great biblical scholars don't realize that grave robbing was very prevalent at the time of Christ. The Bible is referring to not messing with the dead bodies. I also ask them if they've ever heard of the Holy Ghost, stressing the word "ghost." While I have no doubt that the scriptures started out as the word of God, man certainly had quite an influence on it through the last 2,000 years, including omitting gospels.

During one of our sessions mentioned earlier, we had a General Guide by the name of Augustine (as in St. Augustine) come to us and he indicated a willingness to answer tough questions. I explained that I was having trouble answering our critics and asked the best way to handle such negativity. His answer to the question was:

It is written in the Bible what is and is not acceptable. Read Corinthians.

He caught me off-guard with that answer. It had been quite a while since I had read Corinthians, so I thought I would push ahead with the questions. "Do we have the approval of God to do as we do?"

This God does not give approval. If one is of God, that is sufficient.

On that note, my confidence in what we were doing increased exponentially.

On several occasions, we have been honored to communicate with our pastor from the church we attended when we lived in Florida. An incredible man of God, Peter passed away several years ago. The last time he communicated with us on the Spirit Board, I asked him if he was still doing God's work. His answer was:

Always.

I find it very hard to believe that responses like this are the work of the Devil and frowned upon by those in Heaven.

In the past, man has interpreted religious icons in their own image. For instance, in reality, Christ was a Palestinian with dark skin and black hair. In Western cultures where the majority of individuals are Caucasian, Christ is usually depicted with white skin and blond or brown hair. These Western cultures required some kind of image to keep its sinners in line and paying regular visits to the collection plate. The general consensus among the religious leaders evolved that a guy with a red suit and horns would be quite effective. If the conjured up image of the Devil was not sufficient, the added concept of burning in eternal fire was also a very effective weapon in the religious arsenal.

In our previous channeling sessions, the Spirit Guides informed us that they were Heaven-bound spirits and relied upon the energies of Heaven. Who else would be better informed to let us know if there really was a Hell than a heavenly guide? One evening in February 2011, the guides began the session by saying:

So what do you want to talk about tonight?

This was the opportunity I was waiting for so I asked the question: "Is there a Hell?" Everyone in the room waited in silence for the answer to the question.

The question must have been a bit of a curve ball for the guide because there was a hesitation on the board. Slowly the glass began to spell the answer.

O.K., yes, O.K., yes, well kind of?

The Spirit Guide was deep in thought and at a bit of a loss for words. If his statement of "well kind of" was the end of his answer, this was going to be a really short story. Thankfully, the glass began to move rapidly across the board and I breathed a sigh of relief. At least I didn't upset the guides so that they gave up conversation for the night.

Starting with Death

A logical starting place for the guides was death. After all, if you are going to find out if there is indeed a Heaven or Hell, the first step is departing this life. Here is the exact quote telling what they had to say about death.

Death is what you think it is. If you believe in an angel and a pearly gate, then that is what you get. If you believe in fire and men with tails and horns, then that is what you get. If you believe in nothing, then nothing is what you get. Now, at some point, you are going to start asking questions like why am I here and where am I, anyway. And then someone tells you that you do not have to be here.

The glass pointer stopped and then started again by spelling out:

Now Hell is usually saved to scare sinners and free thinkers. To be in Hell, there must be a devil and do you see any?

A mental image immediately came to mind of the guy in a red suit with a long tail and a pitch fork that I'd mentioned earlier, generally with fire in the background. I looked around the room and certainly did not see any present.

Now the guide was getting down to serious business! As a child, I had accompanied my grandparents to tent revival services, where the ministers preached of fire and brimstone for sinners. My distinct memories of the fear of a Hell and the Devil are still clear in my mind. The Spirit Guide had nailed the classic concept of Hell, sinners, and the use of fear. In the many years that have passed since those childhood revival days, I have observed a lot of evil, but I have not personally seen the Devil. I have been told to "go to Hell" on many occasions, but I think that is another issue. Apparently, the Spirit Guide had never seen the Devil either—and I take that to be a good sign.

The next thing the guide said was:

*We all go to the same place. We first judge
ourselves and then we have our loved one judge. If you have
a religion, then they judge you, but mostly you judge yourself.*

I had read about a review of your life taking place soon after passing, but this was the first time our guides spoke of the process. It was becoming more obvious that there was an awful lot of judging going to take place after passing over. There might not be a Hell, but the soul will pay for life's transgressions in other ways.

It seems all recently deceased spirits participate in a review of their lives in which they will witness the pain and suffering they have caused during their time on earth. If you followed your Karma path and led a loving and decent life, your review will be relatively short and you can move ahead with the process of being reunited with your soul family. If on the other hand, you caused a lot of pain and suffering in your incarnate life, your review will be a bit unpleasant. My guess is the vast nothingness referred to earlier is the payback for those who created a lot of suffering in their lives.

The next statement by our Spirit Guide kind of put things into perspective.

O.K., Heaven is a dimension. Yes, almost physical.

At this point, things were moving along nicely. We had confirmation that there was a Heaven that is a dimension and there was apparently no Hell. At least the revival ministers were half right!

Locating Heaven

Have you ever noticed that when Heaven is mentioned, the first impulse is to look toward the sky. One evening, about six months later, we were channeling with a 15th century monk and started to ask questions about Heaven. His message was:

*Another secret teaching, Heaven is visible, it is not
up in the sky, it is the sky. Different dimensions within.*

I responded by trying to grasp his message, asking if he was saying that spirits were all around us, but in a different dimension. The monk replied:

God created the sky and the earth, yes, universe.

His words reinforced earlier messages of the guides concerning the dimension of Heaven.

Carol Green's book *You! And Your Board of Guides*, consists mainly of the transcripts of hundreds of hours of channeling sessions on a Spirit Board. Several of the questions and answers from her book reinforce our current transcripts.

In the mind of each newcomer to our side there is a way to view his or her life. They do this to see the good or the bad in the life past. He judges his own life, for we know the hardest judge is you and you are the most understanding. The criterion for judging own lives is love, understanding, learning, pride, and willingness.

It appeared that the ministers are correct in the fact that there is indeed a judgment day. From the conversations we have with the guides, it looks like the bad are not immediately dispatched to the fire and brimstone of Hell, but undergo an intense judgment of their recently passed life, which can last a very long time.

Carol's book gives us a confirming statement from one of her channeling sessions over thirty years ago.

The Devil is an evil story made up by man to scare little kids and it got out of hand.

It appears that the early preachers and priests were opportunists who jumped on the concept of the Devil. The story worked so well that it was magnified through the ages to the point of universal acceptance.

As the guides ended our current conversation about "Hell," they summed it up with the following statement:

There is good and evil. There is love and hate. There is happy and sad. But there is only Heaven.

Who is Who?

If there is only Heaven, the red guy with horns and a tail is truly a figment of the man's imagination.

As we became more proficient with spirit communication on the talking board, we had the opportunity to delve deeper into the afterlife. One evening the chance arose to ask questions on another subject area related to the Devil: Satan. In Christian teachings, he is an angel that rebelled against God, whose ultimate goal is to lead individuals away from the love of God. In certain circles, Satan and the Devil are synonymous. If there is no Devil, maybe Satan really does not exist. In my mind, there were multiple unanswered questions.

The question of whether Satan truly exists was answered one evening when we had a General Guide, who identified himself as "Augustine," return to a second session with Barbara Lee and me. His profound answers at our previous session had aroused my curiosity, so I mentioned that there was a famous Saint Augustine from the 4th century and inquired if we were talking to the spirit of the great Catholic leader. The reply came back:

I am, yes.

Born in 354 AD, Saint Augustine is acknowledged as one of the great teachers of the word of God and was elevated to sainthood by the Catholic Church after being credited with several miracles. Who better to ask about Satan?

I started by asking if Satan was an actual form that could be seen. His answer was:

Satan is an energy. Lucifer is seen and is the persona of the devil.

I inquired if Satan, Lucifer, and the Devil are all the same thing. His answer was:

No, Satan is another term for Lucifer.
The term devil is a meaning for negative energy.

Since the Devil only exists as a term for negative energy, this answer reiterates the previous answers relating to the Devil being non-existent.

The introduction of Lucifer inserted another concept into the equation. For those of you not familiar with Lucifer, he was an archangel heavily adorned with jewels and finery that was created by God. It would seem that he had quite an ego and was cast out of Heaven because he considered himself better that God. He is also known as the Prince of Darkness. Apparently, he has been trying to get even with God since getting the Heavenly boot.

Next I asked if Lucifer walks the earth. His reply was:

In many forms.

My follow-up question inquired if Lucifer could possess individuals, to which the Saint replied:

Possession is a state of mind.

The horrible Sandy Hook tragedy in Connecticut where twenty young children and six adults were killed had just taken place, so I asked if the person committing the crime was possessed by Lucifer. His answer was quite emphatic:

Lucifer himself does possess what transforms in energy.
Negative energy. Lucifer himself does not possess. Must be clear.

I implied from that statement that only Satan can possess human souls with his negative energy.

Next, I inquired as to the best way to avoid negative energy, to which he replied:

Avoid Satan at all costs.

My next question was: "How do you avoid Satan?" and the spirit of St. Augustine replied:

Think God.

Barbara Lee and I are definitely on the right track when we open each session on the Spirit Board with a prayer that no evil or negative energy attempt to come forward during our efforts to receive messages from the Spirit Guides.

I asked Augustine what, in his opinion, was today's best example of Lucifer on our current culture? His answer was:

The biggest risk is Satan and those who follow him, false prophets, the spreading of negative energy; it will continue unless defeated.

When I asked the identity of the false prophets, his answer was:

Those who teach in all capacities who do not believe in the almighty.

What We Know

When I started this chapter, I thought it would be relatively simple. Now that I have been working on it for over six months and making many changes as the guides provide more information, I can assure you this is a really complex subject. As I now understand it:

- There is no place of fire and brimstone known as Hell.
- There is however, a place in Heaven that it is best to avoid. It is a place of darkness and without contact with other spirits.
- Evil people are definitely treated differently on the other side.
- There is also no Devil running around with a pitchfork and red suit. The image was quite effective in scaring children, but the red suit is only a myth. I know from personal experience that as a child, the picture was quite vivid in my mind. That pitch fork looked like it was quite sharp with barbs and would definitely hurt.

Now for the bad part!

- Satan exists and is very real in the form of a negative energy. He has the ability to possess individuals with this negative energy in the earth plane.
- Lucifer is a follower of the negative energy of Satan. When I asked Augustine about Hitler, his reply was: "he was a follower of Lucifer." My guess is Adolf will be spending an awful long time in the vast nothingness over there. Can you imagine how long it will take for him to pay his karmic debt?

Afterlife: What Really Happens on the Other Side

As the Heavenly guides have pointed out on various occasions, life is a constant battle between good and evil. My guess is that when humans were given free will, the ground work was laid for moral disappointment. As more people turn away from religious teachings in our secular society, fewer people are capable of resisting the negative energy of Satan by thinking God. I believe the dark place in Heaven can hold an unlimited number of souls that have or will respond to the negative energy of Lucifer, or if you prefer, Satan.

Chapter 23
The Big Picture

This final chapter is an attempt to summarize the major aspects of what I have learned about the afterlife. Forgive me if I repeat myself, but I want to reiterate what I feel are the most important lessons. I must confess to having rewritten this chapter several times as my knowledge of the other side has grown. Each time I think it is finished, another door of information is opened at one of our sessions. The more you experience the afterlife from this side of the veil, the more you realize just how much there is to learn about the heavenly structure. Since starting on this learning journey, spirit guides and earthbound ghosts have been spoon feeding me information from multiple sources. Quite often, I am given just enough information at a time to peak my curiosity.

In regards to humans, we live in a three- dimensional life plane. When we talk about the dimensions of the afterlife, things start to get very complicated! We have been told that heaven actually has seven levels or dimensions without time as we know it. I believe that these dimensions are the realms the guides talk about. As the soul gains experience and moves on, it goes to a higher plane or realm. The lowest plane is reserved for those who have led a life of evil. It is also my understanding that a soul can be confined to this lower realm for a very long time.

Heaven is a Slinky
One evening, the spirit guides tried to enlighten us about those dimensions. The words below are the exact message of the spirit guide:

It is not true levels. All are spiraled together. Heaven, life, ghosts, all 7 are separate, but joined. Ghosts are their own. Heaven and god guides, dead being born are all packaged on one dimension. Life all on one. Ghosts on one. Other life experiences on theirs. For now, we are dealing with these 3, heaven, life, ghosts. These 3 are closely located on the slinky. These 3 are easy to travel between. They are energy friendly. But all 7 can be visited and communicated with. Ghosts are not a true dimension; they are kind of stuck. We call this between. They live between the two real dimensions of life and heaven.

At times, the more they try to explain the afterlife details, the more complicated it gets. I must admit I never thought about the dimensions in the afterlife as a slinky. No one ever said learning about life after death was going to be easy.

If At First You Don't Succeed, Reincarnate

The concept of reincarnation is fundamental to understanding what happens after death. We have been told by master guides that it was actually included in the secret teachings of Christ and removed from the Bible in the 1400s. It has been a topic of conversation throughout this book. Upon death, your soul and spirit pass from the life plane, or your incarnate life. At some time in the future, the spirit and soul, should you so choose, are reincarnated into another life on earth.

It's Up To You

This process takes place many times as the soul learns and progresses. When I asked if the soul determines when it wants to reincarnate, the answer was:

*If more experience or lessons are required.
However, it is always the soul's choice.*

Apparently, we have free will on both sides of the veil. In our session with Ulysses Grant, he informed us that he was preparing to reincarnate, but his wife Julia, was not returning. She'd had enough of the aggravation on this life side of the veil. Their ability to look into the future may have had something to do with her decision. I even inquired if two souls can decide to marry in their next lives while they are on the other side. The reply was:

If they so desire.

My wife, Connie, and I have always felt we were soul mates. One evening, I asked the guide how many lifetimes we had been together and I almost fell on the floor when he said:

5 or 6.

This statement gives real meaning to the term "soulmates."

The ongoing course of events in the plane of life takes place under the watchfulness of a hierarchy of guides, saints, angels, and gods. There is actually a chain of command over there that helps tend to your spiritual needs while here on earth. However, the help of the guides may not be available when the soul is on the other side. One evening, I asked if the guides associate with the souls when they are on the other side and the answer was:

We do not visit the lower realms unless we are given a specific mission.

Guides can assist spirits in the lower realms only in special instances. One evening, I asked an earthbound spirit if they communicated with the guides and the reply was:

No.

My assumption is that if the soul occupies the lower realms, only learning and experiences in their incarnate lives allows the soul to advance to the higher realms. Saints and other high achievers in the eyes of God would occupy the highest realm. Their outstanding incarnate life gives them elevated status in the afterlife. The desire to advance is what leads the soul to make the decision to return.

During your time on earth, the soul and spirit have free will to pursue their own ends. Even though you have free will, events are molded by the suggestions of the guides. We generally get into trouble when the heavenly guidance is ignored. I asked if the soul has the ability to choose a life of evil prior to being reincarnated and the answer was:

The choice to be evil is not made here.
Rather a soul may become evil by earthly associations.

The choice to pursue evil will also assure a quick trip to the lowest realm upon death.

When It's Your Time

When you enter the incarnate plane, there is a predetermined end time to your life. I think of it as a round-trip ticket with the return ticket stamped with a time and date at time of birth. One evening, I asked a master guide if the time of death is predetermined by the soul before reincarnation. He spelled out:

Death is written and the soul must abide.

Whenever we inquire into why a person has passed, the answer is "it was his time." I asked if the soul can change its mind and pass prematurely. The guide replied:

Only in early life or by desire to bring about death.

When a child dies in the womb or an unexplained crib death, the soul has changed its mind. I inquired if suicide caused people to die before their time and the answer was:

Most often, yes.

The guides also feel quite strongly about abortion. When I asked if abortion affected the chosen life path of an unborn infant, the answer was:

That is why killing in the womb is not and should
not be accepted. It interferes with a soul journey.

The Soul and the Spirit

All humans have a form of energy called a soul. Many believe that a soul is eternal and passes directly to heaven upon death. Conversely, there are those that believe a soul can also go directly to hell. As you have read in this book, my experiences lead me to other conclusions.

A soul will pass between the death and life planes many times, as it will be re-incarnated in different human body forms. When not in the life plane, the soul will reside in a dimension that is overseen by an all-knowing God. The Deity is assisted by a hierarchy of assistants such as Angels, Saints, Guides, and a variety of other spiritual forms. The goal of the soul while in the life plane is to learn love and cooperation. Upon death, the soul will have its life reviewed to see how it fulfilled the goals. There is a lower realm in the afterlife where persons who did evil in their lives are sent and they will relive their transgressions. In addition, they must ask forgiveness from the harmed individuals.

Listen Closely

Humans can hear from the heavenly guides in a wide variety of ways. Examples of heavenly communication include that little voice of your conscience telling you not to perform an act, writing a book when you have little literary ability, or getting a "bright" idea. There are many ways to receive message from your spiritual helpers. There have been times when I have been in danger and a voice in my mind alerted me to what was about to happen. I will often receive messages in the semi-consciousness that exists just before you wake up in the morning. Many have developed the ability to receive such messages through meditation and some persons are born with the ability to communicate using their mind's eye.

Individuals who can't seem to get the words of the guides on their own may get messages through a clairvoyant or have the words of the message spelled out in detail on a talking board. My first direct contact with the spirit guides came in a channeling session on a talking board in Utah, which I described in Chapter 3. The information gained in that channeling session was instrumental in my present journey of learning about the spirit world.

The Soul and The Spirit

Just as the reader is starting to understand the concept of the everlasting life of the soul, I want to point out that there is a difference between the spirit and the soul. While the soul is in heaven, the spirit can remain in the plane of life as an earthbound ghost. During a channeling session in February 2011, the guides attempted to clarify the difference between the spirit and the soul:

> *Spirit is a spirit, is a spirit, yes. Spirit can travel in any space it chooses to. It has no entrapments, only self imposed. This is why a person can astro-trip. The spirit is not really confined to a body. Yes, spirit is what a ghost is. Its soul is home in heaven. Its spirit chooses to stay in the living.*

A spirit can be a ghost that resides between life and heaven. The intelligent hauntings at Golden Lane are examples of spirits that choose to stay in the living.

In the case of earthbound spirits or ghosts, there are actually two dimensions, referred to as channels by the guides. One such channel is that of the knowing dead. These are the spirits that regularly communicate with us at our various sessions. The other channel is that of the unknowing dead. Our best contact with the unknowing dead is described in Chapter 17, Still Fighting. How it is determined what spirit goes to which channel is beyond my present understanding. I can tell you with certainty that those two channels exist as we have communicated with spirits in both dimensions.

Upon death, the spirit and soul energy will pass from the body and all pain and suffering will be gone. Its incarnate body is left behind with no future use, other than fertilizer. According to many accounts, the soul's guardian angel, friends, and deceased family members will meet the released spirit and the soul upon the act of passing. They will begin the journey through the tunnel that will have a bright white light at the end. As the journey progresses, the soul is accompanied by deceased loved ones, including pets, who will also assist in the passing and getting the newcomer accustomed to their new heavenly surroundings. At our sessions, we have contacted the spirit of deceased family members that have returned for the explicit purpose of assisting an individual who was about to pass. When Steve Jobs, the CEO of Apple Computer, passed, his final words were: "Oh wow, oh wow, oh wow." In my readings, I ran across a transcription from a guide that stated:

Dying is easy; it is the living that is hard.

Another quote from a guide that comes to mind is:

It is those who do not believe in an afterlife that fear death the most.

When a person dies, a soul and spirit still have strong links to the life plane. When they die suddenly, many cannot actually believe they are on the other side. Spirits on the other side miss their remaining loved ones. In our sessions, we receive messages of continuing love and affection for the living who were left behind. A spirit may remain behind to help a loved one through their time of grief. On some occasions, a spirit may be reluctant to leave a prized possession. (This is one of the reasons why antique galleries have a large spirit population.) In instances of sudden or traumatic death, such as being killed on the battlefield, the soul may feel a strong sense of anger or unfinished business. It can make a decision not to pass through the tunnel and remain in the life plane as an earthbound spirit or ghost.

Perhaps these are the spirits that remain in the channel of the unknowing dead. This is why battlefields are some of our most haunted locations. The ghosts of soldiers make some of the strongest apparitions. One evening, I had a soldier spirit throw a small stone at my truck because they did not want me in that location. Another one followed me in the woods and had enough weight to actually break a twig.

It is the earthbound spirits that open doors, can be heard walking on floors, and the ones whose voices we hear over our ghost box at Golden Lane Antique Gallery. I believe the spirits have the option of going to the light of heaven at any time and continuing the journey to rebirth. In one channeling session we were told to tell our child ghost that she had a choice and could decide to move on. Maybe child ghosts need a little more direction.

Spiritual Aids

While the soul and spirit visit the life plane in an incarnate form, there are a multitude of spiritual aids available. Each soul is assigned guardian angels that attempt to protect the individual from time of conception. The baby is also assigned a variety of guides that help them to grow and mature. Most children are born with the ability to communicate with the various spiritual entities. As they grow older, the ability diminishes as mental blocks are formed in the mind. Your guardian angel or guides communicate with you through messages in your mind. The challenge each of us faces is to pay attention to the little voice when it is contrary to the actions we have planned in our mind.

In addition to your guardian angel, there is an entire group of spirit guides available for consultation on various issues. Guides are spirits that have particular knowledge and will share that information if you seek it. They rely on a heavenly energy and are totally independent of any energy assistance from the living. In contrast, earthbound spirits require energies such as a full moon or battery energy. They can also draw energy from living individuals. After our sessions, Barbara Lee and I are often exhausted. In Chapter 5, Meet My Guides, I tell the stories of some of my personal spiritual helpers.

As I mentioned before, all individuals in the life plane have a personal group of guides, whether they realize it or not. They will assist in your daily life, if requested. There is also a hierarchy or pecking order in the heavenly dimension of the guides. Some only deal with special issues. One example is a guide for deceased souls. These spirits are often referred to as gate keepers since they control which earthbound spirits are allowed to get their messages through to the living. It is this guide that helps the earthbound spirits to communicate on the talking board. Whenever we begin a channeling session in which we want to make a specific personal contact, we ask for a guide of deceased souls.

In preparation for sessions concerning special topics, I will often prepare a detailed list of questions concerning the subject. Experience has taught me that when in the presence of an important spirit, such as a past president of the United States, my mind goes blank in the excitement of the moment, so I now come prepared. One night, I had a long list of questions concerning historical conspiracies and requested a special guide. When I asked him if he was aware of the questions I was going to ask, his answer was:

Basically.

On a higher plane, you will find the general guides. General guides carry the messages of the saints and minor gods. They have a far-reaching knowledge and can actually predict the future. One evening, we asked a general guide if he had ever been reincarnated and his reply was that his feet had never touched the earth. Believe it or not, we once contacted a female guide that referred to herself as an apprentice to a general guide. Apparently, promotions must be worked for in heaven just like here on earth.

Another evening, we asked a general guide for whom he was delivering messages. His reply was: Saint Thomas Aquinas. That guide told us that the Pope would retire before his time. We all know how that prediction worked out! In another session, we received a prediction of a miracle. When we inquired the source of the message, the guide replied that it was from the big "C" himself. I will leave the reader to fill in the blanks.

Angel Protectors
In addition to saints and gods, there are also angels that act as messengers of heavenly gods and assist the earthbound spirits. Barbara Lee has an extraordinary ability to communicate with the angels. One evening during a channeling session, we asked the guides to tell us the name of her main angel protector. The board then spelled out the name:

Raphael.

Raphael is an archangel that is responsible for all manner of healing in the Judeo Christian religions. Barbara Lee has dedicated her life to helping lost souls. Her protector is one of the strongest mentors in the heavenly plane.

No living person will know the entirety of what lies ahead after their incarnate life ends. There are definite limits to what we will be told. In a recent session, we asked the general guide a question that could have political implications. The message we received was:

*I cannot at this time. Some things have to follow
their course and not be interfered with.*

There are definitely areas of information that will go unanswered. One evening, I asked how the heavenly guides seem to have all knowledge. The reply was:

Lessons and experiences are unending.

Definitely a good answer, but not quite the information I was seeking. Prior to the presidential election, we inquired into who would be the winner. The answer was always:

It will be close.

As it turned out, their prediction was correct. They will also never give you information for personal enrichment. Lottery numbers are out of the question. Same goes for your time of death. It is preordained and you will not be given information to attempt to change the outcome.

Since free will is allocated to humans, evil exists in many forms. Satan is an energy that can represent himself in many forms. It can possess an individual or a dwelling as discussed in Chapter 14, Protect us From Evil. One evening, we had a guide tell us that war was God's punishment for evil. When asked why believers suffer with the evil doers, the answer was that there must always be sacrifice. Upon passing from this plane, you will be judged and repent for your sins before moving on to your next life experience. The duration of that process is entirely up to you.

If there is one overriding theme that has been presented to us during the hundreds of hours of communicating with the guides, it is that we are entering a time of turmoil and change. When we asked what can be done to get us through what is about to happen, the statement was:

Rely on faith. God knows and is watching and the people will have to help themselves before he will intervene.

Another guide gave us a similar message:

Prayer is important. Believers in God will win. Death is inevitable. Your soul is everlasting. Free choice will determine the journey taken by your soul through the ages.

In Conclusion

In this chapter I have attempted to summarize the wealth of information that has been made available through the various details supplied by the spirits and guides. Our gift of spirit communication has been given to us for a reason. We have been given a glimpse into the afterlife and a clarification of our karma to tell others about the miracles that lay ahead for us all.

I would like to thank the reader for joining Barbara Lee, Connie, and I on this incredible journey. As long as we use the gift for the work of God, I have confidence that our messages will be forthcoming and we can continue down this path of learning.

Bibliography

Asandra. *Contact Your Spirit Guides*. Schiffer Publishing, Atglen, PA 2011
Buckland, Raymond. *The Spirit Book*. Visible Ink Press, Canton, MI 2006
Cayce, Edgar. *Reincarnation and Karma*, A.R.E. Press, Virginia Beach, VA 2005
Green, Carol N. *You! And Your Board of Guides*. Salt Lake City, UT 1981
Weiss, Brian L. *Many Lives, Many Masters*. Touchstone, NY, New York 1988

Other Resources

www.afterlife101.com, *Afterlife 101*
www.afterlifedata.com/ *Afterlife Data*
www.afterliferesearch.weebly.com, *Afterlife Research Center*
www.secretsinthewind.com, *Secrets In The Wind*
www.spiritspredict.com, *Spirits Predict*